DAVID MAINSE

ANSWERS
Your Questions

100 HUNTLEY STREET
25 40
CROSSROADS

SPECIAL ANNIVERSARY EDITION

DAVID MAINSE ANSWERS YOUR QUESTIONS
SPECIAL ANNIVERSARY EDITION
by David Mainse
Published by Crossroads Christian Communications Inc.
1295 North Service Road
P.O. Box 5100
Burlington, ON L7R 4M2
Website: www.crossroads.ca

Unless otherwise quoted, all Scripture quotations are from the Holy Bible, New King James Version. Copyright © 1982 Thomas Nelson Inc.

Scripture quotations marked KJV are from the King James Version of the Bible.

Scripture quotations marked NIV are from the Holy Bible, New International Version. Copyright © 1973, 1978, 1984, International Bible Society.

Scripture quotations marked NLT are from the New Living Translation. Copyright © 1996 Tyndale House Publishers Inc., Wheaton, IL 60189.

Copyright © 2002 by David Mainse. All rights reserved.
Cover/Interior Design: Cathleen Kwas
Editor: Tom Gill
ISBN: 0-921702-92-2

Printed in Canada

DEDICATION

This book is lovingly dedicated to the faithful partners of Crossroads/*100 Huntley Street*. Throughout these many years of ministry, you have touched countless lives and have given them new hope through Jesus Christ...the ultimate "Answer" to their questions. You are appreciated!

TABLE OF CONTENTS

Introduction 13

Part One   MARRIAGE AND FAMILY 15

What does the Bible say about
marriage? 17

How can I help my children make
Godly decisions? 19

What does the Bible say about divorce? 21

I'm divorced but want to remarry.
What does the Bible say? 23

My marriage is in shambles, and I'm
considering separation. Is that Biblical? 25

My husband isn't a believer. How can
I share Christ with him? 27

My husband is physically and emotionally
abusive to both our daughter and me. He will
not go for counselling. Should I divorce him? 29

My wife constantly flirts with other men and
avoids me sexually. While she doesn't sleep with
other men, she does act with lust toward them.
Is this the same as adultery? If so, do I have
grounds to divorce her? 31

My husband isn't a Christian, and I am
constantly unhappy in our marriage. I've tried
to witness to him, but he refuses to listen. Is it
time to give up and just divorce him since I am
unequally yoked to him?. 33

My wife and I just received the Lord. We've
lived common law for several years but have
never formalized our marriage. What does the
Bible say?. 35

My brother has hurt me deeply.
How can I get past the pain?. 37

I'm a new Christian, but my family and friends
aren't saved. I love them but don't want to go
back to my old life. What can I do?. 39

Part Two   SALVATION. 41

My brother says he doesn't need to be saved.
What can I say to him?. 43

I've strayed away from the Lord.
Am I still saved?. 45

I did many bad things in my life before
I received Jesus as my Saviour. How can
I be free of the guilt of my past? 47

Sometimes I don't feel saved.
What should I do? 49

Where did sin originate?
Did God create it? 51

What does it mean to be sanctified? 53

Is water baptism necessary? 55

What is the baptism of the Holy Spirit? 57

How can I know that I've been saved? 59

Part Three   EVERYDAY LIVING 63

Is homosexuality and lesbianism a sin?
If so, why? 65

If God loves us, then why is there evil
and suffering in the world? 67

How can I "keep the faith" in the midst
of my dire circumstances? 69

How do I know that God loves me? 71

What can I do to fight temptation? 73

How can I rid my mind of
impure thoughts? 75

I'm not on the mountaintop; I'm in the valley.
Why does God seem to lift me up only to let
me go back down? 77

What does God say about suicide? 79

I suffer from depression. How can I
break its vicious cycle? 81

Part Four   THE SCRIPTURES 85

How can I know that the Bible is true? Is it
really the Word of God? 87

Why are there so many translations of the Bible?
Is one better than the others? 89

I'm a new Christian. What can I do to
understand the Bible better? 91

What are the "seven deadly sins"?
Why are they deadly? 93

Why does the Bible say
women should be silent? 95

I'm a woman and confused about what to wear.
Should my head be covered?
What about my hair? 97

What was Paul's thorn in the flesh? 99

How can I grow daily in my knowledge
of the Word of God? 101

Cults misuse the Bible. How can I know
if someone is teaching false doctrine? 103

Table of Contents

Part Five   THE AFTERLIFE 109

What are the judgement seat of Christ
and the great white throne of judgement?
Are they the same? 111

What is hell? Is it a real place? 113

What is heaven? Who will go there? 115

What is the difference between the kingdom
of God and the kingdom of heaven? 117

Who are the 144,000 mentioned in
the book of Revelation? 119

What is the new covenant? 121

The Crossroads Ministry Story. 123

Crossroads' Mission Statement. 124

The Crossroads Ministry 125

24-Hour Prayer Ministry. 126

Crossroads Prayer Lines 127

The Geoffrey R. Conway School of Broadcasting
and Communications 128

Circle Square Ranches 129

Crossroads' Emergency Response
and Development Fund. 130

The Walk of Faith 130

Other Crossroads TV Outreaches Sharing
the Love of Jesus 131

Visit The Crossroads Centre 132

INTRODUCTION

This anniversary book is the result of answering countless letters with questions over the past 40 years of ministry at *100 Huntley Street*. I'm grateful to everyone who trusted me enough to ask questions, and grateful to the Holy Spirit for His guidance in answering them.

As you read these questions and answers, I want you to understand a very important truth: Every believer has the same Spirit of truth living inside who yearns to answer questions! Jesus said His Holy Spirit would guide us into all truth (John 16:13). We just need to ask Him the question. Nevertheless, I'm honoured that I may be used by God to be a voice of the Spirit in your lives.

Don't ever stop asking questions. They are the lifeblood to continuing development and growth in the Lord. Furthermore, questions lead to discovery, and discovery leads to fulfillment.

My prayer, along with everyone at *100 Huntley Street*, is that your quest for the Lord and His truth will never wane. God bless you.

Part One

MARRIAGE AND FAMILY

Sing to God, sing praise to His name,
extol Him who rides on the clouds—
His name is the LORD—
and rejoice before Him.
A Father to the fatherless, a Defender of widows,
is God in His holy dwelling.
God sets the lonely in families,
He leads forth the prisoners with singing;
but the rebellious live in a sun-scorched land.
Psalm 68:4-6 NIV

What does the Bible say about marriage?

The Bible speaks very clearly about the roles of men and women and the part each has in God's overall master plan for mankind. It's not by chance that we've been separated into two different sexes, but through God's loving kindness, divine wisdom and knowledge of what we need.

Man was created first by God. Woman was created for man to be his friend, helpmate and lover throughout life:

> *Adam said: "This is now bone of my bones and flesh of my flesh; she shall be called Woman, because she was taken out of Man." Therefore a man shall leave his father and mother and be joined to his wife, and they shall become one flesh.* Gen. 2:23,24

Paul admonished husbands to *"love your wives, just as Christ also loved the church and gave Himself for her"* (Eph. 5:25).

Thus we can see that the husband and wife relationship is very important to the functioning of the body of Christ here on earth. We can also see that this relationship affects our relationship with God and our fellowship and communion with Him.

Peter declared, *"Likewise you husbands, dwell with them with understanding, giving honour to the wife, as to the weaker vessel, and as being heirs together of the grace of life, that your prayers may not be hindered"* (1 Pet. 3:7).

God also has given wives special instruction and guidelines that must be followed. Look at these traits of a virtuous woman:

Who can find a virtuous wife? For her worth is far above rubies. Strength and honour are her clothing; she shall rejoice in time to come. She watches over the ways of her household, and does not eat the bread of idleness. Her children rise up and call her blessed; her husband also, and he praises her. Charm is deceitful and beauty is vain, but a woman who fears the Lord, she shall be praised. Prov. 31:10,25,27,28,30

The heavenly Father's desire is that we live together in peace and harmony. He is our loving Creator and has given us principles and promises from His Word to promote peaceful, loving relationships between husbands and wives. *"Therefore what God has joined together, let not man separate"* (Mark 10:9).

How can I help my children make Godly decisions?

As parents, we want our children to experience God's best in their lives. However, there comes a time when, after we have done our best to raise them for the Lord, they must make their own decisions. This can be very disturbing, especially when we see them making choices that have potentially harmful consequences.

God takes our role as parents very seriously. Therefore, we must take it seriously as well. Remember, God came to earth as a baby, born of Mary. Jesus was raised by earthly parents and was taught by them just as we teach our children today. If God didn't trust the process, He wouldn't have used it Himself!

God's desire is to partner with you in the raising of your children. He is the perfect Father and is willing to share with you all you need to know to grow in perfection as well.

With the Holy Spirit guiding you, you'll make Godly choices yourself. Through that example, your children will see the value of engaging God in all that they do.

One of the most important areas of training up a child is integrity. When children are taught not to lie or cheat, it's a good thing. However, when they see lying and cheating on the part of the parent who taught them, it invalidates all that's been learned. If you want your child not to lie, then don't lie yourself. If you want your child not to cheat, then don't cheat yourself.

Whether you realize it or not, you are being watched very closely by your children. You are the adult example that will impact them the most. What kind of role model are you? Honest? Fair? Loving? Or are you dishonest, unfair and unloving?

Commit your children to God in prayer. Because you are a

believer, your children are sanctified and holy (1 Cor. 7:14). Therefore, God has set His hand to guard and protect them. Remember, it isn't His desire that any should perish but that all come to Him (2 Pet. 3:9).

No matter the age of your children, even throughout the turbulent teenage years, you can count on the faithfulness of God's Holy Spirit to go with them until they make a full surrender of their hearts and wills to the Lord.

Take hold of this encouraging promise from the Lord:

Train up a child in the way he should go, and when he is old he will not depart from it. Prov. 22:6

Then PRAY! PRAY! PRAY!

What does the Bible say about divorce?

F irst let me say that God upholds marriage. It was the first "ordinance" given to man and is as old as humanity itself. It's God's intent for all who marry to stay married.

According to the Scriptures, divorce is wrong. When Jesus was asked about it, He simply stated the positive truth that God made one man and one woman in the beginning (Matt. 19:4,5). Jesus gave us the Biblical basis for divorce in Matthew 5:31-32:

> *Furthermore it has been said, "Whoever divorces his wife, let him give her a certificate of divorce." But I say to you that whoever divorces his wife for any reason except sexual immorality causes her to commit adultery; and whoever marries a woman who is divorced commits adultery.* Matt. 5:31,32

Though God hates divorce (Mal. 2:16), Jesus said it is allowed because of the hardness of man's heart (Matt. 19:8). Let me quickly assure you that all have sinned and come short of the glory of God (Rom. 3:23). Furthermore,

> *If we confess our sins, He is faithful and just to forgive us our sins and to cleanse us from all unrighteousness. If we say that we have not sinned, we make Him a liar, and His word is not in us.* 1 John 1:9,10

There is no need for the "innocent" party to feel guilty. God will forgive the guilty party too, when they repent. The sin of divorce is not the unpardonable sin even when obtained in disobedience to

God's Word. Nevertheless, it must be confessed as any other sin. God is merciful, and as Jesus said to the woman caught in adultery, *"Neither do I condemn you; go and sin no more"* (John 8:11).

God hates divorce because of the heartache and pain it causes to the husband, the wife and in particular the children, who often suffer the most throughout their entire lives. There are always consequences to disobedience. The only thing to do is to accept God's forgiveness and go on with life.

If you are considering divorce, be very careful to separate your feelings from the facts. Has your spouse been unfaithful sexually? Divorce isn't something you enter into because you don't love your spouse anymore. Love is a decision. The feeling of love comes only after the decision has been made. Therefore, decide to love your spouse. Decide to give yourself to him or her.

One of the greatest joys I've had is to remarry several couples who were divorced from each other, came to Christ, began a new life, and decided to love each other. It's clear from Scripture that prayer changes things (James 5:16).

I'm divorced but want to remarry.
What does the Bible say?

I've written many personal letters about this, but because of the possibility of being misinterpreted, I've never published a detailed statement of my position on divorce and remarriage until now. Even the Apostle Paul wrote concerning divorce and remarriage: *"I, not the Lord, say..."* (1 Cor. 7:12). Obviously, Paul was giving his personal opinion and did not claim to speak for God in these few sentences. God says over and over that His mercy endures forever.

Furthermore, the Apostle Paul said, *"This is a faithful saying and worthy of all acceptance, that Christ Jesus came into the world to save sinners, of whom I am chief"* (1 Tim. 1:15). John the apostle said in 1 John 1:8, *"If we say that we have no sin, we deceive ourselves, and the truth is not in us."* There is never a time that any of us can claim to have *no* sin. However, what we can claim is that our sins are *forgiven.*

We must remember what sin is. Both the Hebrew and Greek words translated as sin, carry the meaning of missing the mark or missing the way. Therefore, sin is anything less than thinking the perfect thoughts of God, speaking the perfect Word of God or doing the perfect deeds of God. Never has anyone, other than Jesus Christ, at any time in his or her life lived in such perfection. Therefore, persons who remarry while their original spouse is still living must trust, as all of us do, in the grace of God.

Jesus said that if one divorces for any reason except marital infidelity, and then marries another, it's adultery (Matt. 19:9). Furthermore, we know that adultery is a sin and something in which we must not be involved.

We know that God hates divorce (Mal. 2:16) and hates adultery

(Exod. 20:14). Therefore, we must be very careful not to cross the proverbial line in the sand and simply move from one marriage to another. Examine your divorce. Why did it happen? What is different in you now compared to then? What will you do to ensure the success of this marriage? Most of all, pray. Let the Holy Spirit guide your decision.

My marriage is in shambles, and I'm considering separation. Is that Biblical?

Most ministers avoid giving advice on this subject. The reason for their reluctance is manifold, but mostly centred around the idea that they are only hearing one side of the story.

There are occasions where separation is not only necessary, but is strongly advised. This includes situations where physical violence is present and a person is threatened with harm or even death. Other situations may involve drugs, alcohol, illegal activity, etc.

Though not specifically addressed in the Bible, separation is a tool that can be used to bring a marriage back into proper alignment with God's Word. Unfortunately, many who separate are only looking for an excuse to begin seeking another partner, which is no reason to separate.

My advice to anyone looking at separation is to carefully weigh the situation. Ask these questions:

- Why do I want to separate?
- What do I hope to achieve through separation?
- What do I want for my husband/wife in this?
- Am I willing to be reconciled with my spouse?
- Is the situation dangerous?
- If so, will separation minimize or escalate the danger?

After you've answered these questions and still find separation to be the only alternative, be sure to keep the door open for healing and reconciliation. Also, I urge you to seek advice from a qualified Christian counsellor or pastor to help you and your spouse find a resolution to your problems.

No matter how painful your marriage separation, God is sovereign and can bring good out of this severe trial in your life. If you will allow it, this situation can release you to a fuller commitment to Jesus Christ as Lord of all areas of your life.

Jesus said,

> *But seek first the kingdom of God and His righteousness, and all these things shall be added to you. Therefore do not worry about tomorrow, for tomorrow will worry about its own things. Sufficient for the day is its own trouble.* Matt. 6:33,34

Further reading: Psalms 25:1-22,27; 139:1-12

My husband isn't a believer. How can I share Christ with him?

The issue of a nonbelieving spouse is as old as Christianity. In fact, the Apostle Paul wrote:

And a woman who has a husband who does not believe, if he is willing to live with her, let her not divorce him. For the unbelieving husband is sanctified by the wife, and the unbelieving wife is sanctified by the husband. 1 Cor. 7:13,14

This Scripture is one of hope for you! Paul said that your husband is sanctified through you. This means that he's been set apart for God's purposes because you are his wife.

We know from reading the account of Cornelius in Acts 10 and the account of the Philippian jailer in Acts 16 that God is interested in entire households coming to the saving knowledge of Him.

And he brought them out and said, "Sirs, what must I do to be saved?" So they said, "Believe on the Lord Jesus Christ, and you will be saved, you and your household." Acts 16:30,31

Knowing that God wants your spouse to be saved enables you to pray through the tough times till he comes to Jesus. However, some encouragement is in order. Therefore, here are some points to remember as the spouse of someone who has not yet believed or accepted Jesus Christ as Lord and Saviour:

✓ Don't argue about religion with your spouse. It's absolutely fruitless. Spiritual things can only be spiritually discerned (1 Cor. 2:14; 2 Tim. 2:14).

✓ Submit to your husband in your home as much as possible (Eph. 5:21-24). This action may be a way of showing love and respect (1 Pet. 3:1).

✓ If children are involved in a marriage, they should be taught to love and respect both parents.

✓ Resist the temptation to be resentful or to indulge in self-pity. They are both destructive to your spiritual growth. Find constructive ways to deal with your feelings and emotions, and remember that God understands. He is with you.

✓ Remember to pray for God's strength and for a daily, fresh infilling of the Holy Spirit to help you grow spiritually.

✓ Pray for the salvation of your husband.

✓ Remember, each and every day will have its own troubles (Matt. 6:34), but the Lord promises His ever-abiding presence (Ps. 139:7-13; Isa. 43:1,2).

My husband is physically and emotionally abusive to both our daughter and me. He will not go for counselling. Should I divorce him?

The most urgent thing to consider first is your immediate safety. If your husband is physically abusive, remove yourself and your daughter from the situation immediately. If you have other family members who can provide you a safe place to stay, contact them without delay. If not, seek refuge in a shelter for abused women in your area.

It is not God's will for you to be in a marriage filled with emotional and physical violence. His will is for both you and your husband to love and honour each other and serve Him. Therefore, I cannot tell you whether or not to divorce your husband. However, I can counsel you on steps to take to bring healing to you and your daughter.

You mentioned that your husband would not go for counselling. Will you? Often change begins because one of the partners is willing to step out and seek the help he or she needs. By choosing to separate for safety reasons, an important first step has been taken. This shows your husband two very important boundaries you've put in place:

1. You will not continue to be abused, nor will you allow your daughter to be abused.
2. You are prepared to take strong measures to ensure your safety.

Nevertheless, it's important for you to begin healing so that your family can begin healing as well. By taking first steps, you move toward a resolution instead of remaining stuck in neutral.

Some important questions must be answered in your mind as well, because the answers will determine how you respond to what God does. Answering these questions beforehand also prepares you to receive what God has for you and for your family.

✓ Do you love your spouse? Are you willing to forgive him?
✓ Are you willing to change in whatever ways God shows you?
✓ Are you willing to stay in the marriage if he changes?
✓ Are you willing to do what it takes to save your marriage?

These are tough questions, but they must be answered. Furthermore, your willingness to change may well be the catalyst that starts the entire process of reconciliation and healing. Paul wrote in 2 Corinthians 5:18,19 that, as a Christian, you are a minister of reconciliation. This ministry applies to all aspects of your life, especially your relationship with your husband.

I encourage you to take the steps mentioned. Get your mind clear before you make any life decisions like divorce. But most of all, seek the Lord. Let Him work on both your husband and you. Finally, remember that the prayer team here at *100 Huntley Street* and I are willing to pray for you. *(Please note the prayer line numbers on page 127.)*

My wife constantly flirts with other men and avoids me sexually. While she doesn't sleep with other men, she does act with lust toward them. Is this the same as adultery? If so, do I have grounds to divorce her?

Your situation is unique because it's the wife, not the husband, who is bound by lust. While it's not rare, most situations like yours involve a husband with a roving eye who has lost his desire for his wife.

Nevertheless, the same truth applies. Jesus made it very clear in Matthew 5:28, *"But I say to you that whoever looks at a woman to lust for her has already committed adultery with her in his heart."* Now, some may say that because Jesus was talking to men about women that it doesn't apply to women. However, I find no basis for that in Scripture. One cannot tie that interpretation to this verse simply because Jesus was talking to a group of men.

Therefore we see that, indeed, when someone—either male or female—looks upon another with lust, that person has committed adultery in his or her heart. This isn't the same as the physical act itself, but it is the violation of trust and infidelity in the heart that Jesus is referring to.

So, is it grounds for divorce? I'm not convinced it is. However, it definitely is grounds for some serious counselling, ministry, repentance and forgiveness.

God hates divorce (Mal. 2:16). His perfect will is for a couple to honour each other and treat each other with respect, love, and devotion. Therefore, every effort must be made to save the marriage. Just because one has legal grounds doesn't mean it's the best thing to do.

You've told me about your wife, but what about you? How have you contributed to this tragic situation? Have you withheld yourself from your wife in the past? Have you entered into sexual sin through pornography or habitual self-gratification? Have you been distant from your wife because of your career or personal interests that don't include her?

I challenge you to discover the part of this problem that is yours and begin immediately to correct it. Your wife has lost her affection for you. Help her get it back by devoting yourself to her and deciding to love her through this desperate trial in both your lives. Finally, keep your eyes on your first love, Jesus Christ. He will empower you to love her despite the damage that is done. Read Hosea chapter 3 and see how God can use even this to draw you both closer to Him and each other.

My husband isn't a Christian, and I am constantly unhappy in our marriage. I've tried to witness to him but he refuses to listen. Is it time to give up and just divorce him since I am unequally yoked to him?

U nhappiness in marriage is usually due to more than one factor. While I agree that your unhappiness in marriage may be due in part to the fact that your husband isn't saved, it probably goes far beyond that single issue.

Furthermore, what did Paul mean about being unequally yoked? And does that give you the grounds to cast him out? Let's look at these questions and see what can be gleaned from the Scriptures about your situation.

Paul wrote in 2 Corinthians 6:14 not to be unequally yoked with unbelievers. However, that statement was a general declaration to the church in Corinth to live in harmony with each other.

However, Paul gave very specific instructions in 1 Corinthians chapter 7 to husbands and wives married to unbelievers:

> *If any brother has a wife who does not believe, and she is willing to live with him, let him not divorce her.*
>
> *And a woman who has a husband who does not believe, if he is willing to live with her, let her not divorce him.*
>
> *For the unbelieving husband is sanctified by the wife, and the unbelieving wife is sanctified by the husband; otherwise your children would be unclean, but now they are holy.*

> *But if the unbeliever departs, let him depart; a brother or a sister is not under bondage in such cases. But God has called us to peace.*
>
> *For how do you know, O wife, whether you will save your husband? Or how do you know, O husband, whether you will save your wife?* Cor. 7:12-16

This passage is very clear. Having an unbelieving spouse is not grounds for divorce! Instead, having an unbelieving spouse opens the door for God to do a wonderful work!

How can you know the future? How can you determine whether or not your spouse will ever be saved? Begin to claim by faith his salvation. Press into the Lord to see him saved. As God's desire is for all to be saved, do your part on behalf of your husband. Ask God to give you more love for your husband than ever before, and demonstrate that love with affection—emotionally, physically, and in other practical ways.

During this time of loneliness and despair, deepen your prayers for yourself and your husband. God is bigger than your husband's sin—Jesus proved that—and bigger than your husband's objections as well. Let the Holy Spirit move over the darkness of your husband's soul and speak life and light into him.

My wife and I just received the Lord. We've lived common law for several years but have never formalized our marriage. What does the Bible say?

Prior to receiving Christ, some people become involved in situations that violate God's law. Common law "marriage" is one of them.

Marriage is so important that it must be solemnized in a ceremony. Consider this:

- The first miracle of Jesus happened at a wedding ceremony (John 2:1-11).
- Many of Jesus' parables and stories were about a bride and bridegroom.
- The apostles Paul and John used the illustration of husband and wife to teach about Jesus and the church (Eph. 5; Rev. 21:2).

Fornication is sexual intercourse between partners who are not married to each other. Adultery is voluntary sexual intercourse between a married person and a partner other than the lawful spouse. So the question is: What determines a "spouse"?

A spouse is one with whom you've entered into covenant to live together as husband and wife till death. This usually happens in a legal ceremony before a clergyman and gathered witnesses. God is the third person in your marriage, with the Holy Spirit acting as the glue that binds you together.

Jesus loves you with an everlasting love. Because of this love, He solemnly warns against sexual sin such as fornication and adultery. Hebrews 13:4 states: *"Marriage is honourable among all, and the bed undefiled; but fornicators and adulterers God will judge."*

It's wonderful to know that even though God denounces sin, He provides a way of cleansing and forgiveness. John affectionately writes: *"My little children, these things I write to you, that you may not sin. And if anyone sins, we have an Advocate with the Father, Jesus Christ the righteous"* (1 John 2:1).

Concerning marriage, Jesus said that *"at the beginning [the Creator] 'made them male and female,' and said, 'For this reason a man shall leave his father and mother and be joined to his wife, and the two shall become one flesh.' So then, they are no longer two but one flesh"* (Matt 19:4-6a). Furthermore, Proverbs 18:22 states: *"He who finds a wife finds a good thing, and obtains favour from the Lord."*

I encourage you to solemnize your marriage covenant as soon as possible. It's God's way.

My brother has hurt me deeply.
How can I get past the pain?

I can sense the frustration and hurt you are experiencing from your question. People do hurt others, even those closest to them.

Sadly, Christians often judge one another when they shouldn't. Paul wrote in Romans 14:12,13:

> *So then each of us shall give account of himself to God. Therefore let us not judge one another anymore, but rather resolve this, not to put a stumbling block or a cause to fall in our brother's way.*

Let me share a few thoughts that are based on the Word of God that should help you.

Love is the oil that keeps this universe running. As God's children, we can have the assurance of His love and presence in our lives. Romans 8:38,39 declares that nothing shall be able to separate us from God's love.

The Apostle John wrote that *"We love Him [God], because He first loved us"* (1 John 4:19). Jesus said the two most important commandments are:

- Love God with all your heart, soul, mind and strength (Matt. 22:37).
- Love your neighbour as yourself (Matt. 22:39).

Even when others are unkind to us, it is our responsibility to allow God's love to flow through us to them. Paul wrote in

Colossians 3:13 that *"even as Christ forgave you, so you also must do."*

It's very important to forgive those who have wronged you because the act of forgiveness sets your spirit free from any bondage to resentment or bitterness—two poisons that affect your relationship with Jesus. Remember Christ also suffered unfair judgement, so He can help you have His attitude.

Paul said in Galatians 1:10, *"For do I now persuade men, or God? Or do I seek to please men? For if I still pleased men, I would not be a servant of Christ."* We are responsible to God, and it is He who judges our walk before Him. Any time you compare yourself to others or seek to please men, you take your eyes off Jesus and lower them. Then instead of reaching for the ideal, you stand in danger of reaching for an idol.

You may not know how to forgive your brother. Just ask Jesus. He knows how to forgive those who betrayed and turned against Him. Remember Peter?

I'm a new Christian, but my family and friends aren't saved. I love them but don't want to go back to my old life. What can I do?

Your new life in Christ enables you to love your unsaved family and friends even more than before. This new, deeper love will focus your desire to see them saved. You always desire the best for those you love, and Jesus is the very best.

We all have the need for Christian friends. Sometimes it's hard to make friends in a church we've just begun attending because there may be some "cliques" or tight-knit circles that are closed and hard to penetrate. However, there are always open people who will embrace you in any Holy Spirit-filled congregation. *"A man who has friends must himself be friendly"* (Prov. 18:24a).

The first thing to remember is that as a child of God, you can have the assurance of His love and presence in your life. Paul declared in Romans 8:38,39 that nothing is able to separate you from God's love. He is the *"friend who sticks closer than a brother"* (Prov. 18:24b).

Because of God's great love for you, your self-esteem can be based on Him, not on your past or what others think of you. Often, when one first comes to Christ, worldly friends and family put down the name of Jesus and all who follow Him.

To love the Lord and allow His love to shine through you are two of the most wonderful and important privileges and responsibilities you have as His child. Even when others are not as friendly to you as they should be, it is your responsibility to love and be friendly to them. This action often sparks a new friendship, which can become close and precious. Earnestly pray that you will draw close to the

Lord and will be as He desires you to be.

Jesus said to love your neighbour as you love yourself (Matt. 22:39). In fact, you show your love for God in how you treat your neighbour.

Making new friends is always risky and somewhat daunting. Nevertheless, you must make new friends if you want to grow. This is true in all areas of life, not just the church. However, when you make new friends, choose them carefully. Consider these questions:

Will this new friend...

- help or hurt your walk with God?
- encourage you or debase you?
- lift you up or drag you down?
- help you fulfill your destiny or pull you away from your destiny?

No friend who is true will do anything intentionally to hurt you. Likewise, you wouldn't do anything intentionally to hurt them. Seek relationships that are mutually rewarding and stimulating, leading you both toward your destiny in Christ.

Part Two

SALVATION

For God so loved the world that He gave His only begotten Son, that whoever believes in Him should not perish but have everlasting life. For God did not send His Son into the world to condemn the world, but that the world through Him might be saved. John 3:16,17

Here is a trustworthy saying that deserves full acceptance: Christ Jesus came into the world to save sinners—of whom I am the worst. But for that very reason I was shown mercy so that in me, the worst of sinners, Christ Jesus might display His unlimited patience as an example for those who would believe on Him and receive eternal life. Now to the King eternal, immortal, invisible, the only God, be honour and glory for ever and ever. Amen. 1 Timothy 1:15-17 NIV

My brother says he doesn't need to be saved. What can I say to him?

It's always tough when family and friends deny their need of a Saviour. However, their denial does not remove their need. The Bible clearly teaches that *"it is appointed for men to die once, but after this the judgement"* (Heb. 9:27). The Bible says, *"He who wins souls is wise"* (Prov. 11:30). Pray fervently for wisdom. Jesus promised if you ask for wisdom, you will receive God's wisdom.

When Adam chose to sin rather than to follow God's commandments, physical and spiritual death resulted (Gen. 2,3). Paul wrote in Romans 3:23 that *"all have sinned and fall short of the glory of God."* On our own we can never measure up to God's sinlessness. Paul further wrote that *"the wages of sin is death, but the gift of God is eternal life in Christ Jesus our Lord"* (Rom. 6:23).

However, God loves mankind so much that He gave Jesus, His only Son, to die and thus pay the penalty of our sins. Through Jesus' death, we can be eternally saved from the "lake of fire." The Bible calls this separation from God "hell."

We are saved to live forever with Him in heaven (John 3:3,16-18; Rev. 20:10-15). Our eternity is determined by an act of our free will. We must accept God's gift of salvation—eternal life in Jesus—before we die. John 3:36 declares, *"He who believes in the Son has everlasting life; and he who does not believe the Son shall not see life, but the wrath of God abides on him."*

Jesus said, *"I am the way, the truth, and the life. No one comes to the Father except through Me"* (John 14:6). Salvation comes as we accept Jesus as our personal Saviour by turning from our own way and deciding to go God's way. Paul clearly pointed out God's way of salvation by saying, *"That if you confess with your mouth, 'Jesus is Lord,' and believe in your heart that God raised Him from the dead, you will be saved"* (Rom. 10:9 NIV). Furthermore, according to John 1:11-13, God gives anyone who receives Christ the right to be His very own child.

When you talk with your brother (or anyone else for that matter) about salvation, discuss with them the finality of death. The next breath is guaranteed to no one, not even him. After sharing the above Scriptures with him, ask if he is prepared to gamble with his eternity, or would he receive the guarantee of heaven from Jesus by simply believing Jesus' promise.

If your loved one is willing to open his life to Jesus, then ask him to pray this prayer of repentance and commitment:

> *Father in heaven, I open the door of my spiritual heart to receive Jesus Christ as both my Saviour and Lord. I believe His blood was shed to pay the penalty for my sin so that I might be forgiven and cleansed. Come in right now, Lord Jesus. Cleanse me from every sin and make me a whole person, complete in Your truth and love. God be merciful to me a sinner. Having confessed my sin, I believe You have forgiven me and set me free. Amen.*

If your loved ones need someone to whom they can confess Jesus with their mouth, have them call our prayer lines *(numbers listed on page 127)*. Someone who cares deeply about your loved one will answer the telephone.

I've strayed away from the Lord. Am I still saved?

T he question of whether it's possible for a person to lose their salvation has been debated for centuries. There are many passages of Scripture that I could quote which would seem to support both sides, but I believe we find a beautiful balance in 1 John 1:5-10 (NIV):

> *This is the message we have heard from Him and declare to you: God is light; in Him there is no darkness at all. If we claim to have fellowship with Him yet walk in the darkness, we lie and do not live by the truth. But if we walk in the light, as He is in the light, we have fellowship with one another, and the blood of Jesus, His Son, purifies us from all sin.*
>
> *If we claim to be without sin, we deceive ourselves and the truth is not in us. If we confess our sins, He is faithful and just and will forgive us our sins and purify us from all unrighteousness. If we claim we have not sinned, we make Him out to be a liar and His word has no place in our lives.*

I am no man's judge. Therefore, I can't determine whether you or anyone else is saved. That judgement is reserved for the Lord. God told Samuel that *"...the Lord does not see as man sees; for man looks at the outward appearance, but the Lord looks at the heart"* (1 Sam. 16:7).

If you have accepted Christ as Saviour and are sincerely trying to please God, you will willingly yield control of your life to Him. There are areas of life where changes must be made, so you must be willing to cooperate with God in the maturing process that He has prescribed.

Therefore, take this opportunity to return to Jesus Christ. Remember, He is the One who in great love gave His life so you can live in newness of life with Him. Please bow your head and pray this prayer with me:

Heavenly Father, I come to You now in the name of Your Son, Jesus. Father, I ask You to forgive me of my sins and cleanse me through the blood of Jesus. Help me to live the kind of life You want me to live. I reach out to You in faith with the full realization that without faith, it is impossible to please You. Thank You for receiving me back into Your precious family and thank You for Your wonderful love. In Jesus' name, amen.

I did many bad things in my life before I received Jesus as my Saviour. How can I be free of the guilt of my past?

Y ou were created for a purpose; God has a plan for your life. However, the devil has a plan for your life as well. The Bible says that the devil is a liar and murderer (John 8:44), but it also says,

> *God is not a man, that He should lie, nor a son of man, that He should repent. Has He said, and will He not do it? Or has He spoken, and will He not make it good?* Num. 23:19

The devil only knows your past, not your future. To fulfill his plan for your life, he attempts to thwart the work of God in you by heaping guilt and condemnation on you for what you did before receiving Christ. Know with full assurance that God's purpose in you will be fulfilled: *"...being confident of this very thing, that He who has begun a good work in you will complete it until the day of Jesus Christ"* (Phil. 1:6).

John 8:1-11 records the account of a woman who was caught in adultery and brought before Jesus by the scribes and Pharisees. Unable to withstand Jesus' test of sinlessness, they left *"...being convicted by their conscience"* (v. 9). Jesus gave the woman the seemingly impossible command to *"go, and sin no more."* What He actually did was demonstrate His great love for her by forgiving a sin that was punishable by death under the Jewish law. He also demonstrated that by His power she was now able to quit sinning.

The religious leaders were insincere in their efforts to carry out the Law's prescribed sentence for this woman's sin. They were more concerned about trying to find a way to trap Jesus in His answer to their question.

Jesus did not condone her sin, but instead offered forgiveness and freedom from condemnation that only He could give. Christ still offers the same forgiveness and freedom today. On your own, you can never fully meet the demands of the Law, but through Christ's death on the cross, you have forgiveness of sin. *"For the law was given through Moses, but grace and truth came through Jesus Christ"* (John 1:17).

Call to mind this important verse when past failures and past sins threaten to bring condemnation to your mind and heart: *"If we confess our sins, He is faithful and just to forgive us our sins and to cleanse us from all unrighteousness"* (1 John 1:9). Notice that John was writing to followers of Jesus and that he included himself. If John needed this assurance, so do you.

Paul declares in Romans 8:31, *"If God is for us, who can be against us?"*

Sometimes I don't feel saved. What should I do?

As Christians, we don't always feel saved. This question then must be asked: "Are these feelings correct?"

Feelings are an inadequate test for truth. They fall short because they can change as rapidly as the situation changes. For example, a child being held in the loving arms of a parent feels secure and loved. A moment later, the child is scolded because of disobeying the parent. Now the child's feelings are hurt and the feeling of love and security is absent. However, we know that the child is just as loved and is just as secure as before. The child's feelings are hurt, not his position in the family.

The same is true regarding our position with God. We came to Him through Jesus' sacrificial death and resurrection. Therefore, our position is sure and our forgiveness is secure. Jesus saw to it about 2000 years ago at Calvary.

God's Word is true, and His Word says in Ephesians 2:8,9:

For by grace you have been saved through faith, and that not of yourselves; it is the gift of God, not of works, lest anyone should boast.

Take special note that this does not say by feelings you have been saved—you are saved by faith. Simply trust in the infallible finished work of Jesus, and praise God because you don't have to trust your feelings.

If you invite someone to be a guest in your home, do you repeatedly go to the door to invite him or her in when they are already inside? Of course not! It is the same with Jesus. When you sincerely invite Him into your life, He is anxious to enter and abide. You don't need to repeatedly invite Him to come in; you just accept by faith that He is living within you and that in Him is found complete salvation.

Jesus said, *"If anyone loves Me, he will keep My word; and My Father will love him, and We will come to him and make Our home with him"* (John 14:23). This promise of Jesus is key if you desire to overcome feelings of being unsaved. Do you love Him? If so, then He is with you, right inside your very being.

Praise the Lord for His ever-abiding presence within you!

Where did sin originate? Did God create it?

God created the world and all that is in it. This beautiful story of creation is documented in Genesis chapters 1 and 2, and covers the creation of Adam and Eve, the first human beings on earth. God created everything in His perfection and pronounced it good, including our first parents, Adam and Eve.

Adam and Eve were created in God's image and likeness. Let's read Genesis 1:26,27:

> *Then God said, "Let Us make man in Our image, according to Our likeness; let them have dominion over the fish of the sea, over the birds of the air, and over the cattle, over all the earth and over every creeping thing that creeps on the earth." So God created man in His own image; in the image of God He created him; male and female He created them.*

God is not sinful. Therefore, since God created Adam and Eve in His image and likeness, sin was not created or placed in them. However, Adam and Eve were created with a free will. They could choose what to do or not to do. They could, if they chose, disobey God.

God told Adam that he could eat from any tree in the Garden of Eden, except one—the tree of the knowledge of good and evil. God wanted Adam and Eve to learn about good and evil from Him, not other sources. However, the choice was theirs to make.

When Eve was tempted by the serpent (the devil) she freely chose to disobey God and committed the first sin. Likewise, Adam fell into sin when he ate the forbidden fruit.

The devil deceived Eve by telling her she wouldn't die if she ate the fruit. Eve was also told that she would be like God by partaking. Sadly, this tactic of the enemy is still taking its toll today. People are fooled every day into thinking they can be like God. Rather than worshipping the One True God, they focus on themselves and sink lower and lower, farther and farther away from Him.

God's ultimate desire is for a being made in His own image to freely give Him praise. That's why He created us. John wrote, *"You are worthy, O Lord, to receive glory and honour and power; for You created all things, and by Your will they exist and were created"* (Rev. 4:11).

When we, as God's creatures, worship Him, we fulfill an important role in our destiny. We were created to worship God, but sin blocks our relationship with Him.

Seek God today. If you sin, He'll forgive you when you ask Him for cleansing. Then worship Him in spirit and in truth (John 4:23).

What does it mean to be sanctified?

The word "sanctified" is first used in the Bible to describe the setting apart of the vessels and artifacts in the tabernacle of Moses for the purpose of God. We who believe are also set apart for His purposes. Sanctification is the relationship we enter into with God by faith in Christ. It is both a fact as well as a process and is an important, necessary part of Christian life.

When we trust Jesus for cleansing from all sin, we become sanctified or set apart unto God by the working of the Holy Spirit. *"And such were some of you. But you were washed, but you were sanctified, but you were justified in the name of the Lord Jesus and by the Spirit of our God"* (1 Cor. 6:11).

Sanctification is a continual work that takes place in us immediately as we receive Jesus as Saviour and as we make Him Lord through our walk with Him. The Apostle Paul referred to this in Colossians 3:8-12 as he admonished believers to "put off" the old man, which is the sinful nature; and "put on" the new man, which is Christ's holiness and righteousness. He said we are to "reckon" the old man dead. The word "reckon" is a mathematical term, which means to know a fact. We know this fact: We are dead to sin. The faith we exercise to believe that fact is the same faith that releases the power of the Spirit to enable us to live a sanctified life.

As we mature spiritually, we become more like Christ and actually begin taking on His image. Paul wrote in Philippians 3:10-14 about his condition of being not yet perfect, but said that his purpose was to forget what was behind and to *"press toward the goal for the prize of the upward call of God in Christ Jesus."* Complete Christlikeness will finally be realized when *"that which is perfect has come"*

(Christ's return) and *"that which is in part will be done away"* (1 Cor. 13:10).

Jesus told the disciples to wait in Jerusalem until they received *"power from on high"* (Luke 24:49). This power is none other than the Holy Spirit of God. Jesus said, *"If anyone loves Me, he will keep My word; and My Father will love him, and We will come to him and make Our home with him"* (John 14:23). This indwelling of the Father and the Son is personified in the Holy Spirit. Therefore, one cannot help but become more and more like Christ, with Him living inside.

As you pursue God and His righteousness, you'll be confronted with these questions:

- What is the Holy Spirit showing you about your life that needs to be corrected?
- How are you being shaped into the image of Christ?
- What habits, thoughts and attitudes is the Holy Spirit revealing to you that must be discarded?

Your answer and willingness to change determines your walk with God.

Is water baptism necessary?

On the day of Pentecost, Peter stood before a large crowd and preached about Jesus Christ. The Holy Spirit so inspired Peter's words that great conviction fell upon the crowd: *"Now when they heard this, they were cut to the heart, and said to Peter and the rest of the apostles, 'Men and brethren, what shall we do?'"* (Acts 2:37).

Peter's response to this cry of the heart is just as valid today as it was 2,000 years ago: *"Repent, and let every one of you be baptized in the name of Jesus Christ for the remission of sins; and you shall receive the gift of the Holy Spirit"* (Acts 2:38).

It's vital to always compare Scripture with Scripture when arriving at your conclusions. Other Scriptures teach that calling on the name of the Lord will save you and that by believing in Jesus you have eternal life. There's no mention of water baptism in these.

When Jesus was dying on the cross, the thief next to Him said, *"Lord, remember me when You come into Your kingdom."* Jesus replied, *"Assuredly, I say to you, today you will be with Me in Paradise"* (Luke 23:42,43). It's obvious that this man had neither the time nor opportunity to be baptized, but Jesus did not hesitate in assuring him of his salvation. Jesus is the same yesterday, today and forever. He only looks at the heart and is aware of all the circumstances in our lives.

Peter, under the power of the Holy Spirit, declared to a Jewish crowd familiar with baptism, that this outward act testifies to their obedience to God and their new life in Christ. Baptism declares the past dead. The "old man of sin" is gone and is considered dead, drowned in the waters.

Or do you not know that as many of us as were baptized into Christ Jesus were baptized into His death? Therefore we were buried with Him through baptism into death, that just as Christ was raised from the dead by the glory of the Father, even so we also should walk in newness of life. Rom. 6:3,4

Baptism is a symbol of our identification with Christ's burial and resurrection. We testify through baptism that we were in Christ when He was judged for sin, that we were buried with Him, and that we have risen to new life in Him. Water baptism is a confirmation of what has happened to us through salvation.

Jesus instructed believers to *"Go...and make disciples of all the nations, baptizing them in the name of the Father and of the Son and of the Holy Spirit"* (Matt. 28:19). If you've not been baptized, don't delay. This important ordinance empowers you to live a victorious life in Christ.

I pray that you'll receive this word and act on it today. Jesus instituted two ordinances that involve a physical act: baptism and the "Lord's Supper" or communion. Therefore, all who desire to walk in obedience to Christ must be baptized and partake of the Lord's Supper.

What is the baptism of the Holy Spirit?

When a person receives Jesus as Saviour and Lord, that person also receives the gift of the Holy Spirit. He indwells every believer. However, there is a special enduing with power that God has promised as well, which we call the baptism of the Holy Spirit.

The book of Acts gives an accurate and detailed account of the early Christian church. Just prior to Jesus' ascension, He told the disciples to tarry or wait in Jerusalem until they had received power when the Holy Spirit had come upon them (Acts 1:4,8).

The Bible states that about 120 people (Acts 1:15) were gathered together in an upper room, praying and waiting for this promised power to come (Acts 2:1). Suddenly, a sound like a rushing mighty wind filled the room and the Holy Spirit was poured out on those gathered: *"And they were all filled with the Holy Spirit and began to speak with other tongues, as the Spirit gave them utterance"* (Acts 2:4).

After this initial infilling or baptism, we read of other instances where believers received the baptism of the Holy Spirit:

- Acts 8:14-17 states that the Samaritan Christians had received the Word of God (Christ) and were baptized in water, but had not received the full baptism of the Holy Spirit until the apostles laid hands on them.
- Acts 19:6 says this about some believers in Ephesus whom Paul found: *"When Paul had laid hands on them, the Holy Spirit came upon them, and they spoke with tongues and prophesied."* This happened after these believers had received Christ and were baptized in water.

Scripture indicates that one may believe in Jesus but not receive the full baptism of the Holy Spirit. It is the Lord's desire that every believer receive this experience and daily walk in the Spirit (Acts 2:38).

Paul wrote, *"Be not drunk with wine, wherein is excess; but be filled with the Spirit"* (Eph. 5:18 KJV). The word "be filled" should be understood as "be *being* filled." It implies a continuous drinking from God's artesian well of His Spirit. The power of God is given for us to live as Jesus lived and to minister the gifts of the Spirit as Jesus did.

It's my conviction that in these days just before the return of Jesus, we must not settle for anything other than "Book of Acts" Christianity. We must apprehend or take hold of the power that is promised to us as believers and demonstrate to the world that God is alive and active in His creation.

If you've not received the baptism of the Holy Spirit, pray this prayer:

> *Lord Jesus, thank You for promising to send Your Holy Spirit to live in me. I ask You now, Lord, to baptize me with Your Holy Spirit. I receive Your Holy Spirit of Promise now. In Jesus' name, amen.*

How can I know that I've been saved?

One of the beautiful marks of true Christianity is the knowledge of being saved. The Bible tells us that the enemy is a liar and seeks to destroy what God has made. Jesus said, *"The thief does not come except to steal, and to kill, and to destroy. I have come that they [we] may have life, and that they [we] may have it more abundantly"* (John 10:10).

Have you opened the door of your life to invite Jesus to be Saviour and Lord? Be certain of this, because God is deeply concerned about you and wants to give you the assurance of His salvation.

The resurrection of Jesus Christ is the divine assurance that sin has been dealt with to the satisfaction of God's demands. Jesus bore our sins on the cross, and in so doing, put them away forever.

God's Word is what brings quiet assurance as seen in these Scriptures:

> *Bless the LORD, O my soul, And forget not all His benefits.* Ps. 103:2

> *"No more shall every man teach his neighbour, and every man his brother, saying, 'Know the Lord,' for they all shall know Me, from the least of them to the greatest of them,"* says the LORD. *"For I will forgive their iniquity, and their sin I will remember no more."* Jer. 31:34

> *I will greatly rejoice in the LORD, my soul shall be joyful in my God; for He has clothed me with the garments of salvation, He has*

covered me with the robe of righteousness, as a bridegroom decks himself with ornaments, and as a bride adorns herself with her jewels. Isa. 61:10

Assurance of salvation is not for a few days, weeks or months, but forever! It's this blessed assurance that God delights to impart to all who come to Him as needy people seeking the "Way" of life (Isa. 32:17). Let me encourage you to bow your head and pray this prayer:

Heavenly Father, I come to you now in the name of Jesus, Your Son. I realize that I can only come to You through Him. Father, forgive me of my sins and cleanse me through the blood of Jesus. I reach out to You in faith to receive from You the full assurance of salvation that You promise in Your Word. I thank You now in Jesus' name. Amen.

How do you know this has really happened? **Because God says so!** He cannot lie. Jesus said that *"The one who comes to Me I will by no means cast out"* (John 6:37), and *"Behold, I stand at the door and knock. If anyone hears My voice and opens the door, I will come in to him and dine with him, and he with Me"* (Rev. 3:20). *"The gift of God is eternal life in Jesus Christ our Lord"* (Rom. 6:23b).

Please remember that an emotional experience alone is not proof of salvation, no matter how glorious it was. The only proof is the promise of Jesus. You know you're saved because He says so. The cleansing blood of Jesus is what makes you safe (1 John 5:11-13). Ephesians 2:8,9 declares that *"by grace you have been saved through faith."* Notice this doesn't say that by your feelings you have been saved. You are saved by faith. Simply trust in the work of Jesus in His death and in His resurrection. Praise God! You don't have to trust how you feel! You can trust in the Word of God.

I also cannot stress enough the importance of being part of a loving church fellowship where your spiritual growth can be nurtured and your faith strengthened. There are times when we all need the encouragement of fellow Christians, especially when facing the challenges of life. It should be a church where the Word of God is preached in fullness and where the power of prayer is evident.

We trust and pray that the Lord will guide you to a solid church home where you will feel loved and part of God's family. *(If you would like a referral to a church in your area, please contact the Crossroads Ministry Centre. The numbers are listed on page 127.)*

...being confident of this very thing, that He who has begun a good work in you will complete it until the day of Jesus Christ....
Phil. 1:6

Part Three

EVERYDAY LIVING

I beseech you therefore, brethren, by the mercies of God, that you present your bodies a living sacrifice, holy, acceptable to God, which is your reasonable service. And do not be conformed to this world, but be transformed by the renewing of your mind, that you may prove what is that good and acceptable and perfect will of God. Romans 12:1,2

And with many other words he [Peter] testified and exhorted them, saying, "Be saved from this perverse generation." Then those who gladly received his word were baptized; and that day about three thousand souls were added to them. And they continued steadfastly in the apostles' doctrine and fellowship, in the breaking of bread, and in prayers.... Now all who believed were together, and had all things in common, and sold their possessions and goods, and divided them among all, as anyone had need. So continuing daily with one accord in the temple, and breaking bread from house to house, they ate their food with gladness and simplicity of heart, praising God and having favour with all the people. Acts 2:40-42,44-47a

Is homosexuality and lesbianism a sin? If so, why?

The Bible says that God created us in His image and likeness—male and female—and that we are to be fruitful and multiply (Gen. 1:26-27). In order to be fruitful and multiply, both sexes are necessary.

Sex is a gift from God, ordained for one man and one woman within the bonds of holy matrimony. Any sexual deed outside the set standards found in God's Word, whether homosexual or heterosexual, is contrary to God's design and purposes for creating us as male and female. *"Look, this was the iniquity of your sister Sodom: She and her daughter had pride, fullness of food, and abundance of idleness; neither did she strengthen the hand of the poor and needy"* (Ezek. 16:49).

The city of Sodom was destroyed because of materialism and homosexuality. Moses wrote about what happened at the front door of a citizen of Sodom named Lot. Several men had gathered around his home and asked him to bring his visitors out into the streets so that they could abuse them sexually.

Foolishly, Lot offered his virgin daughters to the mob at his door rather than let them near his guests. However, the guests pulled Lot back into the house and *"struck the men who were at the doorway of the house with blindness"* because of their homosexual sins (Gen. 19:4-11).

The prophet Isaiah referred back to Sodom many years later, saying, *"The look on their countenance witnesses against them, and they declare their sin as Sodom; they do not hide it. Woe to their soul! For they have brought evil upon themselves"* (Isa. 3:9).

Paul wrote:

> *For the wrath of God is revealed from heaven against all ungodliness and unrighteousness of men, who suppress the truth in unrighteousness.... God gave them up to vile passions. For even their women exchanged the natural use for what is against nature. Likewise also the men, leaving the natural use of the woman, burned in their lust for one another, men with men committing what is shameful and receiving in themselves the penalty of their error which was due.* Rom. 1:18,26-27

God has great love for everyone, including homosexuals, and has a passionate desire to set each one free from a destructive, perverse lifestyle. Simply hearing the truth, embracing it and repenting, enables anyone bound in this sin to be forgiven. By daily and nightly partaking of the Word of God, by the prayer of deliverance and by continually being filled with God's Holy Spirit, a man or woman is set free. *"And you shall know the truth, and the truth shall make you free"* (John 8:32).

If God loves us, then why is there evil and suffering in the world?

It's true that God loves us. In fact, the Bible says that God loves us with an everlasting love (Jer. 31:3). However, the problem of evil and suffering is still present. Nevertheless, I must first stress that God does not take pleasure in seeing people suffer.

To understand how the issue of evil and suffering came about, we don't have to look far in the Bible. The disobedience of the first man and woman brought sin into the world (Gen. 3). Their nature was altered because of the separation from God caused by disobedience, and this caused all their descendants to be infected with sin (Rom. 5:12).

Along with this sinful nature of man came a host of painful consequences that mankind must endure. The fact of original sin leads to eternal death if not dealt with through God's provision—the shed blood and the death of Jesus Christ. Paul wrote, *"For the wages of sin is death, but the gift of God is eternal life in Christ Jesus our Lord"* (Rom. 6:23).

God is unchangeable, and so are His laws: *"For I am the Lord, I do not change"* (Mal. 3:6a). On our own, we will never totally understand God's ways because God's thoughts and ways are higher, or loftier, than ours:

> *"For My thoughts are not your thoughts, nor are your ways My ways," says the Lord. "For as the heavens are higher than the earth, so are My ways higher than your ways, and My thoughts than your thoughts. For as the rain comes down, and the snow from heaven, and do not return there, but water the earth, and make it bring forth and bud, that it may give seed to the sower*

and bread to the eater, so shall My word be that goes forth from My mouth; it shall not return to Me void, but it shall accomplish what I please, and it shall prosper in the thing for which I sent it." Isa. 55:8-11

God's Word going forth from His mouth (His Spirit) is His thoughts. Think about it!

Consider the magnitude of evil and suffering, and also consider the result. For example, how many people have...

- come to the Lord because of the evil around them?
- learned to depend on God in the midst of suffering?
- reached out to help others in dire need because of disaster, terrorism and war?
- devoted themselves to the plight of those lost in the grip of evil?

No one is guaranteed an escape from pain and suffering, but we have a precious promise in Psalm 46:1 that *"God is our refuge and strength, a very present help in trouble. Therefore we will not fear...."* Therefore, take hold of the promise that God loves you and that in all things He has your very best interests in mind. Then choose to trust Him every single day of your life.

And we know that in all things God works for the good of those who love Him, who have been called according to His purpose. Rom. 8:28 NIV

How can I "keep the faith" in the midst of my dire circumstances?

G od's Word promises that no matter how difficult the situation *"all things work together for good to those who love God..."* (Rom. 8:28). Therefore, we can truly count on the Lord to see us through every experience of our lives, whether on the mountaintop or in the deepest valley.

The night I committed my life to Jesus, I was given the best advice ever:

1. Read at least a few Bible verses every day.
2. Pray every day.
3. Tell somebody about Jesus.
4. Get to church at least two or three times a week.

My counsellor told me that as long as I did these four things consistently, I would not fail in following Jesus. As you devote time to His Word, you'll see the mighty ways He delivered His people and will rest assured that what He did for them, He'll do for you.

One Scripture I recommend is 1 Peter 1:6,7. This passage will bless your life with its assurance of certain victory in any time of grief or trial:

> *In this you greatly rejoice, though now for a little while, if need be, you have been grieved by various trials, that the genuineness of your faith, being much more precious than gold that perishes, though it is tested by fire, may be found to praise, honour, and glory at the revelation of Jesus Christ....*

Joseph provides a beautiful example of one who was severely tried. He was sold into slavery by his own brothers, tempted by his employer's wife, unjustly accused and then thrown into prison for something he did not do. Nevertheless, the Lord was with Joseph. Read his amazing story in Genesis chapters 37-50 and see God's care and faithfulness displayed. Joseph eventually rose to the exalted position of Prime Minister of Egypt.

Job is another wonderful example of the trusting faith that is so precious in God's sight. After experiencing the loss of his health, family and possessions, Job could still testify, *"Though He slay me, yet will I trust Him"* (Job 13:15). Job 42:9-17 reveals how God richly blessed Job after he endured his severe trial. Verse 10 states that *"the Lord gave Job twice as much as he had before."* Truly, God is great!

The Bible says in Romans 10:17 that *"faith comes by hearing, and hearing by the Word of God."* To build up your faith, you must hear much of God's Word. The greatest hindrance to the growth of faith is a lack of knowledge of God's Word. Many people pray to get faith, but faith only comes by hearing the Word of God. To believe God for any circumstance of life, discover what He has to say from His Word and then act upon it. Jesus assures us that *"heaven and earth will pass away, but My Words will by no means pass away"* (Matt. 24:35).

When you read God's Word, He is talking to you. When you pray, you are talking to God. However, it's absolutely essential that you don't do all the talking. The Word says to cast *"all your care upon Him, for He cares for you"* (1 Pet. 5:7).

Even if you don't feel up to it, it's important that you tell another person about what God has done. It may be from the Bible, or it may be from your life or someone else's life. Doing this will immediately encourage you.

Finally, do whatever it takes to either get to church, or if you can't go out, see that the church gets to you.

How do I know that God loves me?

God's love for you is profoundly deep and perfect in every way. You may experience moments in your life when you don't feel loved, but God's love is not founded on the feelings, conditions and limitations of mankind.

The Bible says, *"We love Him because He first loved us"* (1 John 4:19). It's important to realize that God chose to love us freely before we loved Him in return. We can rest in the knowledge of His love regardless of our failures and have peace that we are *"accepted in the Beloved"* (Eph. 1:6).

Paul wrote about the security each believer has in the love of Christ. There was no doubt in his mind as he penned...

For I am persuaded that neither death nor life, nor angels, nor principalities nor powers, nor things present nor things to come, nor height nor depth, nor any other created thing, shall be able to separate us from the love of God, which is in Christ Jesus our Lord. Rom. 8:38,39

"God is Love" John wrote in 1 John 4:16. This amazing verse begins with these words: *"And we have known and believed the love that God has for us...."* Truly, this is not just knowledge acquired through learning about God or even by simply believing what has been written or taught about Him. It comes as the result of receiving Jesus as Saviour and Lord and confessing who He is: *"Whoever confesses that Jesus is the Son of God, God abides in him, and he in God"* (1 John 4:15). The Bible further declares that *"in this the love of God was manifested toward us, that God has sent His only begotten*

Son into the world, that we might live through Him" (1 John 4:9).

God's love is best displayed in the coming of Jesus, the One who loved us so much that He was willing to leave heaven's glory (Heb. 1:6) to overcome Satan (Matt. 4:11) by surrendering His will to the Father (Heb. 10:7). Jesus' love took Him to the cross (John 13:1; Col. 1:20-22) and then brought Him back from the dead (Luke 24:6).

God loves you with an everlasting love (Jer. 31:3). He so loves you that He sent Jesus on your behalf so that you can find forgiveness and redemption in Him. The best way to know that God loves you is to believe Him today. Receive His promise of love, and love Him in return. Love is a decision, and He has already decided to love you. It's your decision to receive the love He has for you.

What can I do to fight temptation?

How can a young man keep his way pure? By living according to Your word. I seek You with all my heart; do not let me stray from Your commands. I have hidden Your word in my heart that I might not sin against You. Praise be to You, O Lord; teach me Your decrees. With my lips I recount all the laws that come from Your mouth. I rejoice in following Your statutes as one rejoices in great riches. I meditate on Your precepts and consider Your ways. I delight in Your decrees; I will not neglect Your word.
Ps. 119:9-16 NIV

The psalmist declared that living according to God's Word enables one to live a pure life. The best example of this principle is Jesus and His temptation in the wilderness (Matt. 4:1-11; Luke 4:1-13). Hebrews 4:15 states that Jesus *"...had the same temptations we do though he never once gave way to them and sinned"* (TLB).

Jesus lived on earth as a human. He laid aside all the privileges of being God and never used His "Son of God" status to help Himself. That's why He always referred to Himself as "Son of Man." Furthermore, Jesus experienced temptation and didn't sin. Therefore, He can help us gain the victory as we rely on Him.

These verses will encourage you:

Because He Himself suffered when He was tempted, He is able to help those who are being tempted. Heb. 2:18 NIV

I can do all things through Christ who strengthens me.
Phil. 4:13

73

Yet in all these things we are more than conquerors through Him who loved us. Rom. 8:37

No temptation has overtaken you except such as is common to man; but God is faithful, who will not allow you to be tempted beyond what you are able, but with the temptation will also make the way of escape, that you may be able to bear it.
1 Cor. 10:13

Take active steps against temptation and prepare yourself for spiritual battle. Submit to God, resist the devil and he will flee according to James 4:7. Take every thought captive and set your mind on the things of the Lord (2 Cor. 10:5; Col. 3:2). Meditate on whatever is true, noble, just, pure, lovely, of good report or praiseworthy (Phil. 4:8). Finally, if you fall, repent. Jesus will meet you there and will forgive you (1 John 1:9).

How can I rid my mind of impure thoughts?

The man, Job, wrote, *"I made a covenant with my eyes not to look lustfully at a girl"* (Job 31:1 NIV). Job decided to guard the main gate of temptation regarding impure thoughts—his eyes. He knew that thoughts derived from lust are degrading to the woman, to the man, and to God.

When you accept Jesus as your Saviour and make Him Lord, you become a new creature in Christ. *"Therefore, if anyone is in Christ, he is a new creation; old things have passed away; behold, all things have become new"* (2 Cor. 5:17). Because of your status as a new creation, you are no longer under the power of sin. The enemy of your soul, the devil, would have you think you can't keep from sinning, but the truth is you're free. You can decide not to sin.

Paul advises:

> *...put off, concerning your former conduct, the old man which grows corrupt according to the deceitful lusts, and be renewed in the spirit of your mind, and that you put on the new man which was created according to God, in righteousness and true holiness.*
> Eph. 4:22-24

He further wrote:

> *I beseech you therefore, brethren, by the mercies of God, that you present your bodies a living sacrifice, holy, acceptable to God, which is your reasonable service. And do not be conformed to this world, but be transformed by the renewing of your mind, that you*

may prove what is that good and acceptable and perfect will of God. Rom. 12:1,2

When impure thoughts return seeking to defeat you, take active steps against them. Take captive every thought and make it obedient to Christ (2 Cor. 10:5). Paul talks about holy living in Colossians 3:1-17. I encourage you to read and meditate upon this Word from God.

Most of all, pray. Prayer is the weapon of choice when dealing with impurity. Prayer puts you on the same page with God as you work through the tangle of twisted thoughts that litter your soul. Day and night seek God's face and seek His purity. When you do, I promise that you'll find freedom in Christ.

I'm not on the mountaintop; I'm in the valley. Why does God seem to lift me up only to let me go back down?

Y ou are going through an experience that is common to most Christians. Like you, many people refer to it as being in the valley rather than on the mountaintop.

We tend to appreciate the mountaintop experiences in life because of the sense of God's closeness and blessing upon us. However, we must remember that though the view from the mountaintop is wonderful, growth takes place in the valley where life-giving streams flow.

We've had guests on *100 Huntley Street* who have told of similar experiences in their lives. After coming through the valley, they realize that they have actually grown closer to the Lord as a result. Looking back over their circumstances, they've been able to give thanks to God for the difficult times because it caused them to search for God with their whole hearts. They have found that God's Word is true:

> *"For I know the plans I have for you," declares the Lord, "plans to prosper you and not to harm you, plans to give you hope and a future. Then you will call upon Me and come and pray to Me, and I will listen to you. You will seek Me and find Me when you seek Me with all your heart."* Jer. 29:11-13 NIV

There is nothing you can do to earn God's love. Likewise, there is nothing you can do to earn your salvation. It is a gift that you receive simply through faith in Christ's finished work on the cross.

Jesus paid the penalty for sin, and you are accepted because of His righteousness (Eph. 1:6,7).

Though your circumstances cause you to feel far from the Lord, your relationship with Him remains secure because it is not based on feelings but on the fact of His unchanging love. You may not understand why you are going through this valley, but be assured that God has not left you. His promise is sure, and His presence is assured. God has said, *"I will never leave you nor forsake you"* (Heb. 13:5).

Valleys are times of testing and trial. Your faith will remain immature and weak unless it's tested. Jesus even went through times of testing and trial: *"...though He was a Son, yet He learned obedience by the things which He suffered"* (Heb. 5:8).

Remember Paul's words of comfort: *"And we know that all things work together for good to those who love God, to those who are the called according to His purpose"* (Rom. 8:28).

What does God say about suicide?

There are no easy answers when it comes to the question of suicide. The Bible has no direct reference to its moral implications, and so it becomes an area where we, as individuals, must seek God's truth through His Holy Spirit.

There are basic truths found in the Bible that we can use to guide us in the right direction. First, we know that death is not the end of our existence, but the beginning of life eternal. For the Christian, it is eternity with God; but for the unbeliever, it is eternity in a place not prepared for human beings but for Satan and his followers.

The Bible mentions certain men who took their own lives. You may find it of interest to examine the lives of these men and discover for yourself what led them to that end.

King Saul killed himself with his own sword (1 Sam. 31:4). His life went steadily downhill after he chose to disobey God by becoming involved in the occult with a visit to a spiritualist or medium. By the time he killed himself, Saul was completely disregarding God, and the Spirit of God had departed from him.

Judas hanged himself after betraying Jesus to the Jewish political/religious establishment (Matt. 27:5), and afterward could not cope with the guilt.

Like murder, suicide is taking life that God has created. Furthermore, it betrays a lack of faith or trust in God. Therefore, we can safely state that it is sinful (Exod. 20:13). Christians can never justify such an act because it goes completely against their confession of surrender and trust in God.

Jesus promised to work all things together for your good if you give every situation over to Him (Rom. 8:28). Your life is a sacred trust before God. He loves you so much, He gave His only Son to die for you on Calvary (John 3:16). Commit your life entirely to Jesus, and let Him live through you (Gal. 2:20) so you will be able to claim His peace and joy (Isa. 26:3; Ps.16:11).

God is a God of mercy. Those who commit suicide in ignorance of God's laws or in a state of mental illness will be judged according to the light that was in them. To whom little is given, little is required; but to whom much is given, much is required.

My prayer for those considering suicide is that God will speak to their hearts and bring peace in the midst of their situation. My wife Norma-Jean wrote a song to the suicidal. I remember how, in the middle of the night, she was troubled and went into a prayer of intercession for precious people about to commit suicide. She left the bedroom and went downstairs to the piano and sang...

When life's not worth the living, and you feel you just can't go on,
No one seems to understand, and everything seems to go wrong,
Don't give in to your feelings, your feelings can go up and down,
Don't take your life but give it, give your life to Jesus Christ.
Don't give up, don't give up, give your life to Jesus.

Don't give up, don't give up, He wants to give you new life.
New life you will receive if you will only believe.
The words that Jesus said, "Come unto Me."

You may feel today rejected, depressed, unloved, alone.
Your life seems all in pieces, your dream all shattered and torn.
There's still hope in One who loves you.
He wants to be your closest friend.
Don't take your life but give it, give your life to Jesus Christ.

Don't give up, don't give up, give your life to Jesus.
Don't give up, don't give up, He wants to give you new life.
New life you will receive if you will only believe
The words that Jesus said, "Come unto Me."

I suffer from depression.
How can I break its vicious cycle?

Depression is often triggered because of adverse circumstances that threaten a person's welfare. Psalm 16:11 says, *"You have made known to me the path of life; You will fill me with joy in Your presence, with eternal pleasures at Your right hand"* (NIV).

God's desire is to deliver His children from periods of depression and fear. Furthermore, God desires to see His children live in victory and not defeat. However, we must be fully surrendered to Christ and His plan for our lives.

Depression turns your thoughts away from God and puts them squarely on you and your problems. Ask God to help you take your mind off yourself and put it on Him. Surrender to Jesus as Saviour and Lord right now if you haven't done so already. It's the beginning of the road to recovery and restoration. Pray this prayer with me now:

> *Dear God, I admit that I am a sinner and need Jesus Christ in my life to become my Saviour and Lord. Right now, I turn over the controls of my heart and life to Jesus. Come into my heart, Lord Jesus, and forgive all my sins. Amen.*

You've just taken the first step to recovery from depression by accepting Jesus Christ into your heart and making Him Lord of your life. *"But as many as received Him, to them He gave the right to become children of God, even to those who believe in His name"* (John 1:12).

Christ alone provides assurance of true love and forgiveness. *"And this is the testimony: that God has given us eternal life, and this life is in His Son"* (1 John 5:11).

"But God, who is rich in mercy, because of His great love with which He loved us, even when we were dead in trespasses, made us alive together with Christ (by grace you have been saved), and raised us up together, and made us sit together in the heavenly places in Christ Jesus" (Eph. 2:4-6).

I cannot overemphasize the importance of total forgiveness. Therefore, make sure you've forgiven everyone who has ever hurt you in any way. Forgiveness is paramount to defeating depression, and you can only forgive yourself after you've forgiven others.

It is God's desire to show you further steps of victory in your life. He does this by giving you His power to resist any satanic thought patterns of resentment or self-pity that threaten to entrap you. *"No temptation has overtaken you except such as is common to man; but God is faithful, who will not allow you to be tempted beyond what you are able, but with the temptation will also make the way of escape, that you may be able to bear it"* (1 Cor. 10:13). God is faithful, and He knows your limitations and cares for you (1 Pet. 5:7).

God will enlighten your mind as you daily read His Word and pray. With His divine love in your heart, you will soon learn to forgive anyone who has wronged you.

Finally, ask the Lord to fill you with His Holy Spirit. The Holy Spirit will remove any defeat in your heart and replace it with a new song of victory (Eph. 5:18-20; Ps. 40:1-3).

Through the years I've asked those suffering with depression this question: "If your physician were to prescribe a pill daily for 30 days for your depression, would you take the pills faithfully?" The answer has always been "Yes."

Then I've said, "If I give you a *spiritual* prescription, will you take it daily for 30 days?" I've never known this prescription to fail in lifting depression. Here it is: "Read the little book of Philippians every day for 30 days and ask daily for the same joy of which Paul speaks."

Remember, Paul was writing to the people in the city in which he and Silas sang praises to God at midnight while in prison.

Please know that our Crossroads prayer lines are available to you 24 hours a day. *(You will find a complete list of them on page 127.)* Our prayer partners are willing to pray with you for God's wisdom, direction and healing as you journey toward wholeness and the abundant life that He so desires for you.

Important Note:
In addition to addressing depression spiritually, you may also want to see your family physician to address possible physiological components, or a Christian psychologist to help you deal with any psychological and emotional factors. Stay free of debilitating depression by maintaining a close walk with God and by living a balanced life – spiritually, physically, emotionally and relationally.

Part Four

THE SCRIPTURES

All Scripture is inspired by God and is useful to teach us what is true and to make us realize what is wrong in our lives. It straightens us out and teaches us to do what is right. It is God's way of preparing us in every way, fully equipped for every good thing God wants us to do. 2 Tim. 3:16,17 NLT

So then faith comes by hearing, and hearing by the word of God. Rom. 10:17

How can I know that the Bible is true? Is it really the Word of God?

Thousands across the ages have asked these questions as they've grappled with belief.

Skeptics would say that the writers of the Bible were on their own. "God was not involved," some say. However, the Apostle Paul wrote in 2 Timothy 3:16, *"All Scripture is given by inspiration of God."*

While each of the 40 writers of the Bible used words and expressions familiar to them and wrote in their unique styles, Scripture (or the Word of God), is a divine product and must be approached and acknowledged as such. God ensured that His thoughts put in human words were what He wanted written.

The Old Testament passages of Moses and the prophets are identified both as spoken and written with God's own speech (Neh. 8; Ps. 119). New Testament writers view the Old Testament as the oracles of God (Rom. 3:2) that were written by men who were moved by the Holy Ghost (2 Pet. 1:21). Christ and His apostles quote Old Testament texts, not merely as what Moses, David or one of the prophets said (Mark 7:9,10; 12:36; Rom. 10:5), but also as what God said through these men.

Furthermore, the contents of the book itself speak to its inspiration. The Bible contains 66 books written by 40 different authors, yet the theme and theology remain intact throughout. No hoax of this magnitude could withstand the scrutiny the Bible has been subjected to over the centuries from both inside and outside the community of faith.

Jesus promised that the Holy Spirit would guide the believer into all truth: *"But when He, the Spirit of truth, comes, He will guide you into all truth"* (John 16:13 NIV). You can have confidence that God will do just what He said He would do—guide you into all truth.

Take the advice of James, the man known as the brother of Jesus, and let God answer for Himself about the truth of His Word:

> *If any of you lacks wisdom, he should ask God, who gives generously to all without finding fault, and it will be given to him. But when he asks, he must believe and not doubt, because he who doubts is like a wave of the sea, blown and tossed by the wind.*
> James 1:5,6 NIV

The Bible is true. It's inspired of God, and it still speaks to us today. Embrace it and you will learn about a heavenly Father who loves you more than you can imagine.

Why are there so many translations of the Bible?
Is one better than the others?

S ome believe there is only one correct translation of the Bible, the King James Version. I enjoy this version a great deal as well, and read and study from it regularly. However, it is important to note that God's Word was originally written in Hebrew, Aramaic and Greek.

Scholars over the centuries have translated copies of the original manuscripts into the languages of their day. This first happened in Alexandria, Egypt, when Jewish Rabbis translated what we call the Old Testament into Greek. Jerome translated the entire Bible into Latin, which became the standard for a thousand years.

In Britain, Wycliffe saw the need for people to read the Bible in their own language, so in 1380 he began the labourious task of translating the manuscripts into common English for the first time. Later scholars in 1611 translated original Greek and Hebrew texts into English, creating what became known as the King James Version.

During the past century, scholars desired to translate the Scriptures from more ancient manuscripts discovered since the King James Version was completed. Another goal was to modernize the language. The original language of the King James Version of 1611 is difficult to understand, though there have been several revisions—approximately one every 100 years. I personally use the New King James Version, translated in the 1970s.

Some paraphrases of the Bible have been done as well, such as *The Living Bible* and *Good News for Modern Man*. Unlike *The Living Bible*, the *New Living Translation* is a recent translation, not a paraphrase. While I use the *New King James Version*, I can recommend the

New International Version and *The Amplified Bible.*

Newer translations solve the language issue, but vary in how the Biblical text is rendered on the page. Examine several and ask the Holy Spirit to guide you to the one that would work best for you. Beware of translations done by any one denomination or cult. The translations I mentioned have scholars of various denominations who watch over each other to ensure the work is not denominationally biased.

Most important of all, **just read it every day and every night.**

I'm a new Christian. What can I do to understand the Bible better?

The golden rule of Bible interpretation is to compare Scripture with Scripture. By following this rule, you will discover that the Bible interprets itself. It's important to understand that the Old Testament is foundational to the New Testament, but the New Testament interprets by the Old. I know this may seem confusing, but as you dig deeper into the Bible you'll see it's true.

For example, Jesus is referred to as the *"Lamb of God"* in John 1:29: *"The next day John saw Jesus coming toward him, and said, 'Behold! The Lamb of God who takes away the sin of the world!'"* To understand what that Scripture means, we must go to the Old Testament for an interpretation:

> *Isaac spoke up and said to his father Abraham, "Father?"*
> *"Yes, my son?" Abraham replied.*
> *"The fire and wood are here," Isaac said, "but where is the lamb for the burnt offering?"*
> *Abraham answered, "God Himself will provide the lamb for the burnt offering, my son."* Gen. 22:7,8 NIV

> *He was oppressed and He was afflicted, yet He opened not His mouth; He was led as a lamb to the slaughter, and as a sheep before its shearers is silent, so He opened not His mouth.* Isa. 53:7

These are just two of many Old Testament passages that lay the groundwork for Jesus as the Lamb of God.

Another foundational principle of interpretation is to study a passage in its larger context. Read carefully the before and after verses, and if you are still perplexed, check with your pastor or Bible teacher and ask for the historical Christian understanding of the passage.

The key to all of this is to maintain a proper Scriptural balance. If you have incomplete information or hold an extreme view in some area of Christian doctrine, you place yourself in danger of being deceived. Truth can be perverted or twisted when something is given greater credence than is found in the Bible. Keep it in balance, *"rightly dividing the word of truth"* (2 Tim. 2:15).

Never stop being a student of Scripture. You'll discover that the depths of God's Word await the hungry student with treasures of truth. God doesn't put truth in the Word to keep it hidden. He has placed it there awaiting discovery by His children. Proverbs 25:2 declares, *"It is the glory of God to conceal a matter, but the glory of kings is to search out a matter."* Luke wrote about believers in Berea, who *"examined the Scriptures every day to see if what Paul said was true"* (Acts 17:11 NIV).

What are the "seven deadly sins"? Why are they deadly?

Solomon lists seven things in Proverbs 6:16-19 that the Lord finds detestable:

1. Haughty eyes (or a proud look)
2. A lying tongue
3. Hands that shed innocent blood
4. A heart that devises wicked schemes
5. Feet that are quick to rush into evil
6. A false witness
7. A man who stirs up dissension among brothers

One of the best ways to understand why these sins are deadly is to consider them in light of whether they bring death or life. Examining each one by itself reveals that these activities all seek to destroy rather than build. Hence their designation as "deadly."

While these sins are considered the deadly sins, all sin is sin. One of the most dangerous things we can do is categorize sin to minimize one or maximize another. All sin leads away from God and His perfect plan for our lives. The Apostle John wrote,

> *We know that we have come to know Him if we obey His commands. The man who says, "I know Him," but does not do what He commands is a liar, and the truth is not in him.*
> 1 John 2:3,4 NIV

John makes it very clear that to truly know Christ is to obey Him. Furthermore, we know that the Law and the Prophets are summed up in one word—*love.* Jesus taught this when asked which of the commandments was the most important (Matt. 22:34-40).

It's wonderful to know that our Lord Jesus took care of all forms of sin for us at Calvary! Isaiah 1:18 declares, *"Though your sins are like scarlet, they shall be as white as snow; though they are red like crimson, they shall be as wool."* When we come to Him with our guilt and sin, He says, *"Neither do I condemn you; go and sin no more"* (John 8:11) because *"He is the atoning sacrifice for our sins, and not only for ours but also for the sins of the whole world"* (1 John 2:2 NIV).

Therefore, *"If we confess our sins, He is faithful and just to forgive us our sins, and to cleanse us from all unrighteousness"* (1 John 1:9). Please notice that John is writing to believers and that he included himself. Don't be discouraged. Do what John did, confess, ask for forgiveness and cleansing, repent with Godly sorrow, and *"Go and sin no more."* God forgives and washes away all sin.

Why does the Bible say women should be silent?

The Bible speaks very clearly about women and their role in the body of Christ. God created both men and women, not just men. Therefore, rest assured that God looks with equal love on women and equips them to fulfill His plan as well.

Paul wrote in 1 Corinthians 14:34 that women should remain silent in the churches. What is not stated is that Paul was dealing with keeping order in the public worship services. To properly understand what Paul said, we must understand the context of the passage and the customs of the time.

At that time, a wall divided the worship area with the women on one side and the men on the other. Some women were in the habit of yelling out questions to their husbands in the middle of the service. This practice interrupted the order and decorum of worship, so Paul was simply asking the women to wait until after the service to ask their questions. A similar passage in 1 Timothy 2:11 addresses the same situation. My father spent 21 years in Egypt where the wall remains, separating women and men. He told me that he has had to ask both women and men to be quiet and speak to each other at home.

Paul instructed Christian women to behave modestly, denoting reverence and respect. He encouraged women to concentrate on their real adornment or Godliness—good works that allow God's love to transform and shine through them.

Don't forget that men are held to a high standard as well: *"...blameless, the husband of one wife, temperate, sober-minded, of good behaviour, hospitable, able to teach; not given to wine, not violent, not greedy for money, but gentle, not quarrelsome, not covetous"* (1 Tim. 3:2,3).

Paul emphasizes the beautiful characteristic of a wife having a teachable spirit and quiet submission to her husband. It also states that a woman is not to usurp authority over a man. Remember to use Scripture to interpret Scripture. Paul also taught, *"Submit to one another [husbands and wives] out of reverence for Christ"* (Eph. 5:21 NIV). Immediately following this statement, Paul addressed the relations between husbands and wives in detail.

Paul, in other areas of Scripture, is pleased to commend the ministry of several women. He mentions, for example, Phoebe (Rom. 16:1), Priscilla (Rom. 16:3,4), Tryphena, Tryphosa and Persis (Rom. 16:12); Euodia and Syntyche (Phil. 4:2,3).

The key to this entire subject is in understanding the role of both men and women and God's desire for His order in the church. Sadly, over the centuries, men have attempted to use these Scriptures as weapons to subdue women. However, Paul clearly stated that men are to love and honour their wives and bathe them in the Word of God, and to present them to God, holy and spotless (Eph. 5:25-27). God loves women with no distinction, just as He loves men.

I'm a woman and confused about what to wear. Should my head be covered? What about my hair?

Any question about dress that we seek to answer from Scripture must take into consideration the time and culture in which the instruction was given. Even today, women in many eastern nations and cultures are required to wear coverings over their hair and often their face as well!

Your question concerning women covering their heads in church most likely comes from what Paul wrote in 1 Corinthians 11:1-16. It's important to remember that the culture and customs of the people Paul was addressing were different than today.

The custom in Greek and eastern cities of that day was for moral women to cover their heads in public. Doing so guaranteed safety and respect in the streets. Some of the Christian women, taking advantage of their new liberty in Christ, began to boldly lay aside their veils when praying in church.

This caused an uproar in the church because the temple prostitutes in Corinth at the time wore no covering and painted their faces. Many of the believers were horrified at such an action. Thus, Paul instructed them to not defy public opinion as to what was considered proper for women in that culture.

The symbolism of head covering for women was important as well. Paul was teaching a spiritual principle that simply stated a woman should be "covered" and not dishonour her "head" by shaving her hair, which may also have been a practice of temple prostitutes.

It was customary at the time of Paul in the Greek and Roman world for women to wear their hair long while the men wore it quite short. Today there is great cultural variety of dress, so we need to keep in mind these verses: *"Let your moderation be known unto all men"* (Phil. 4:5 KJV). *"In like manner also, that women adorn themselves in modest apparel"* (1 Tim. 2:9 KJV).

We should not call undue attention to ourselves by being extremely conservative or extremely loud. Remember, *"whatever you do, do all to the glory of God"* (1 Cor. 10:31).

Paul's last word on the subject to the Corinthians was that they should not be contentious (1 Cor. 11:16).

What was Paul's thorn in the flesh?

And lest I should be exalted above measure by the abundance of the revelations, a thorn in the flesh was given to me, a messenger of Satan to buffet me, lest I be exalted above measure. Concerning this thing I pleaded with the Lord three times that it might depart from me. And He said to me, "My grace is sufficient for you, for My strength is made perfect in weakness." Therefore most gladly I will rather boast in my infirmities, that the power of Christ may rest upon me. Therefore I take pleasure in infirmities, in reproaches, in needs, in persecutions, in distresses, for Christ's sake. For when I am weak, then I am strong.
2 Cor. 12:7-10

It's important to accept Paul's statement as is. Paul's thorn was a messenger of Satan that God permitted so that Paul would remain small in his own eyes. It was said by the prophet Samuel of Saul, the king, *"Although you were once small in your own eyes, did you not become the head of the tribes of Israel? The Lord anointed you king over Israel"* (1 Sam. 15:17 NIV).

Paul wrote of the many times he had been whipped, stoned and left for dead, imprisoned, shipwrecked and other like persecutions in 2 Corinthians 11. God made sure Paul did not become "big" in his own eyes. The smaller a person is in his own opinion, the bigger God can be in his life.

Paul declared that he took pleasure in infirmities, reproaches, necessities, persecution and distresses because when he was weak he became strong (2 Cor. 12:9,10). His weakness kept him dependent upon the Lord and God's sufficient grace, which gave him power to rise above the buffetings of Satan.

I'm not convinced that Paul's thorn in the flesh was anything physical so far as sickness was concerned. When you read Paul's letters to the churches, you'll discover a common thread that runs throughout: his persecution by Judaizers who sought to define the church in the context of the Law.

This faction of believers vehemently insisted that new Gentile believers must be circumcised and observe the Law of Moses. The controversy became so heated that the apostles met in Jerusalem to debate the issue. James addressed the council saying,

> *Therefore I judge that we should not trouble those from among the Gentiles who are turning to God, but that we write to them to abstain from things polluted by idols, from sexual immorality, from things strangled, and from blood.*
> Acts 15:19,20

Jesus gave this advice to Paul regarding the thorn: *"My grace is sufficient for you."* James and the council in Jerusalem supported Paul, and through the council, Jesus set the record straight: Let the Gentiles come! My grace is sufficient for them as well.

How can I grow daily in my knowledge of the Word of God?

Getting to know the Word of God is no different from getting to know anything else—you must spend time with it. Sadly, many Christians spend little or no time in the study of the Word and so are subject to deception and error, or at best, no growth.

Maintaining a regular time of personal Bible study is important. When our physical bodies become hungry for food, we don't wait until we are starving before we eat. We usually schedule our meal times so that we have sufficient nourishment to meet our daily needs. Likewise, we should schedule our Bible reading and study so we are taking in adequate amounts of God's Word on a daily basis in order to meet the challenges of the day.

For this reason, I have constantly published daily Bible reading guides over the years. Our monthly magazine, *Crossroads Compass,* serves this purpose today. We have topical studies nearly every day on the *100 Huntley Street* telecast and also have chapter-by-chapter studies that consistently move through the Word. It is vital to minister the Word publicly every day.

Jesus is the "Word of God" according to John:

> *In the beginning was the Word, and the Word was with God, and the Word was God. He was in the beginning with God. And the Word became flesh and dwelt among us, and we beheld His glory, the glory as of the only begotten of the Father, full of grace and truth.* John 1:1,2,14

Further, Jesus identified Himself as the "Bread of Life":

I am the living bread which came down from heaven. If any-one eats of this bread, he will live forever; and the bread that I shall give is My flesh, which I shall give for the life of the world.
John 6:51

Jesus went on to declare:

Most assuredly, I say to you, unless you eat the flesh of the Son of Man and drink His blood, you have no life in you.... For My flesh is food indeed, and My blood is drink indeed. He who eats My flesh and drinks My blood abides in Me, and I in him.
John 6:53-56

From these Scriptures we can draw a powerful metaphor. As we devour God's Word, it's as if we are feeding on Jesus Himself. When one eats something, every cell in the body derives nourishment from that which is eaten. It is the same with the Word of God in our spirit.

Cults misuse the Bible. How can I know if someone is teaching false doctrine?

All Scripture is God-breathed and is useful for teaching, rebuking, correcting and training in righteousness, so that the man of God may be thoroughly equipped for every good work. 2 Tim. 3:16,17 NIV

A sure way to identify a cult is how they esteem the Scriptures. The following questions can be used as guidelines to help you identify a cult or any particular group whom you may question.

1. **Does the group believe that the Bible is the holy, inspired Word of God, and the only inspired book given according to the following Scriptures?**

   Forever, O Lord, Your word is settled in heaven. Ps. 119:89

   Heaven and earth will pass away, but My words will by no means pass away. Matt. 24:35

   All Scripture is given by inspiration of God, and is profitable for doctrine, for reproof, for correction, for instruction in righteousness. 2 Tim. 3:16

   ...for prophecy never came by the will of man, but holy men of God spoke as they were moved by the Holy Spirit. 2 Pet. 1:21

2. Do they accept any other "sacred" book as equal to or a perfect supplement to the Bible?

3. Do they believe that the only salvation from sin is through the blood of Jesus Christ? Here are two of many Bible statements on this:

> *For this is My blood of the new covenant, which is shed for many for the remission of sins.* Matt. 26:28

> *And according to the law almost all things are purged with blood, and without shedding of blood there is no remission.* Heb. 9:22

4. Do they believe that Jesus died on the cross and rose again on the third day in His physical body?

> *Behold My hands and My feet, that it is I Myself. Handle Me and see, for a spirit does not have flesh and bones as you see I have.* Luke 24:39

5. Do they believe in the virgin birth of Jesus Christ?

> *Now in the sixth month the angel Gabriel was sent by God to a city of Galilee named Nazareth, to a virgin betrothed to a man whose name was Joseph, of the house of David. The virgin's name was Mary.* Luke 1:26-28

> *Therefore the Lord Himself will give you a sign: Behold, the virgin shall conceive and bear a Son, and shall call His name Immanuel.* Isa. 7:14

Now the birth of Jesus Christ was as follows: After His mother Mary was betrothed to Joseph, before they came together, she was found with child of the Holy Spirit...and [Joseph] did not know her till she had brought forth her firstborn Son. And he called His name Jesus. Matt. 1:18,25

6. Do they believe that Jesus Christ is the only way to God?

Jesus said to him, "I am the way, the truth, and the life. No one comes to the Father except through Me. John 14:6

For there is one God and one Mediator between God and men, the Man Christ Jesus. 1 Tim. 2:5

7. Do they believe that Jesus Christ is the Son of the living God?

For God so loved the world that He gave His only begotten Son, that whoever believes in Him should not perish but have everlasting life. He who believes in Him is not condemned; but he who does not believe is condemned already, because he has not believed in the name of the only begotten son of God. John 3:16,18

8. Do they believe that there is only one God, and that there is none other like Him?

To you it was shown, that you might know that the Lord Himself is God; there is none other besides Him. Deut. 4:35

Hear, O Israel: The Lord our God, the Lord is one! Deut. 6:4

9. Do they believe in a literal hell and a literal heaven?

There was a certain rich man who was clothed in purple and fine linen and fared sumptuously every day. But there was a certain beggar named Lazarus, full of sores, who was laid at his gate, desiring to be fed with the crumbs which fell from the rich man's table. Moreover the dogs came and licked his sores. So it was that the beggar died, and was carried by the angels to Abraham's bosom. The rich man also died and was buried. And being in torments in Hades, he lifted up his eyes and saw Abraham afar off, and Lazarus in his bosom.

Then he cried and said, "Father Abraham, have mercy on me, and send Lazarus that he may dip the tip of his finger in water and cool my tongue; for I am tormented in this flame." But Abraham said, "Son, remember that in your lifetime you received your good things, and likewise Lazarus evil things; but now he is comforted and you are tormented. And besides all this, between us and you there is a great gulf fixed, so that those who want to pass from here to you cannot, nor can those from there pass to us."

Then he said, "I beg you therefore, father, that you would send him to my father's house, for I have five brothers, that he may testify to them, lest they also come to this place of torment." Abraham said to him, "They have Moses and the prophets; let them hear them." And he said, "No, father Abraham; but if one goes to them from the dead, they will repent." But he said to him, "If they do not hear Moses and the prophets, neither will they be persuaded though one rise from the dead." Luke 16:19-31

Therefore Sheol has enlarged itself and opened its mouth beyond measure; their glory and their multitude and their pomp, and he who is jubilant, shall descend into it. Isa. 5:14

10. Do they believe that Jesus, being God's Son, is co-equal and co-eternal with God the Father?

Jesus said to them, "Most assuredly, I say to you, before Abraham was, I AM." John 8:58

And now, O Father, glorify Me together with Yourself, with the glory which I had with You before the world was. John 17:5

Father, I desire that they also whom You gave Me may be with Me where I am, that they may behold My glory which You have given Me; for You loved Me before the foundation of the world. John 17:24

I've quoted some Bible passages in answer to the questions posed. These are just a sampling as there are hundreds of other sentences in God's Word which declare God's truth on these matters. It's important to study thoroughly in two ways:

- Topically (everything the Bible says about a given subject)
- Verse by verse

I am determined to help believers in every way I can to study in both the above ways. *"Be diligent to present yourself approved to God, a worker who does not need to be ashamed, rightly dividing the word of truth"* (2 Tim. 2:15).

Part Five

THE AFTERLIFE

And He showed me a pure river of water of life, clear as crystal, proceeding from the throne of God and of the Lamb. In the middle of its street, and on either side of the river, was the tree of life, which bore twelve fruits, each tree yielding its fruit every month. The leaves of the tree were for the healing of the nations. And there shall be no more curse, but the throne of God and of the Lamb shall be in it, and His servants shall serve Him. They shall see His face, and His name shall be on their foreheads. There shall be no night there: They need no lamp nor light of the sun, for the Lord God gives them light. And they shall reign forever and ever. Rev. 22:1-5

What are the judgement seat of Christ and the great white throne of judgement? Are they the same?

The judgement seat of Christ and the great white throne of judgement are two different terms describing two different judgements. The Bible says that everyone will be judged according to what they've done, believers and unbelievers alike. The difference is in where the judgement will take place and before whom each person will stand.

Briefly, the judgement seat of Christ is where Jesus rewards believers for a life lived in Christ. The great white throne of judgement is where God judges unbelievers, because their names are not written in the Book of Life. Let's look at each one in more detail.

The judgement seat of Christ is the throne of Jesus Christ in heaven, where all who are born again and have been redeemed by Jesus' blood will gather to give an account of their stewardship on earth. Paul discusses this in 1 Corinthians 3 and 2 Corinthians 5. Paul wrote: *"For we [believers] must all appear before the judgement seat of Christ, that each one may receive the things done in the body, according to what he has done, whether good or bad"* (2 Cor. 5:10).

For the believer, it's important to remember that we are judged according to what we say (Matt. 12:35-37) and what we do (1 Cor. 3:12-16). Our stewardship is all-encompassing, just as His grace is all-inclusive.

The great white throne of judgement is the final judgement for all unbelievers:

Then I saw a great white throne, and Him who sat on it, from whose face the earth and the heaven fled away. And there was found no place for them. And I saw the dead, small and great, standing before God, and books were opened. And another book was opened, which is the Book of Life. And the dead were judged according to their works, by the things which were written in the books. And anyone not found written in the Book of Life was cast into the lake of fire. Rev. 20:11,12,15

When God looks at one's words and deeds, He's actually examining the heart of that person. Jesus said that out of the heart a man speaks (Luke 6:45). Jeremiah declared, *"The heart is deceitful above all things, and desperately wicked; who can know it?"* (Jer. 17:9).

God desires that none perish but that all are saved (2 Pet. 3:9). Call on Him now. Receive His gift of life before it's too late. Jesus said that *"whoever confesses Me before men, him I will also confess before My Father who is in heaven"* (Matt. 10:32).

I believe that when Jesus heard me confess Him as Saviour and Lord as a 16-year-old, He said to His Father, "There's David Charles Mainse. He's publicly declaring that he believes in Me." I believe the angels heard Jesus and proceeded to write my name in the Book of Life. May everyone make the same confession!

What is hell? Is it a real place?

Hell was created for Lucifer (the devil) and those who follow him. Lucifer rebelled in heaven and drew away one third of the heavenly host. Because these angelic beings chose not to remain with God in heaven, a place was prepared for them to dwell. Jude declares, "And the angels who did not keep their positions of authority but abandoned their own home—these He has kept in darkness, bound with everlasting chains for judgement on the great Day" (Jude 1:6 NIV).

John declared:

> *The sea gave up the dead who were in it, and Death and Hades delivered up the dead who were in them. And they were judged, each one according to his works. Then Death and Hades were cast into the lake of fire. This is the second death. And anyone not found written in the Book of Life was cast into the lake of fire.*   Rev. 20:13-15

Hell is a real place and not a pleasant one at that! Everyone, Christian and non-Christian alike, should be aware that, according to the Bible, there is full consciousness in hell.

Jesus told a story in Luke 16:19-31 about a rich man who died, went to hell and was consciously tormented. This man looked and saw a man named Lazarus who had begged for food from him while they both lived on earth. Lazarus was in a place called "Abraham's Bosom," enjoying eternal life with the Lord while the rich man was in Hades being tormented. Make no mistake; this story was not a parable because God's Word was so specific as to name an actual person, Lazarus. I do not believe Jesus would use specific names and places if it were not an historical fact.

Hell was not created for human beings. The Bible says that hell was prepared *"for the devil and his angels"* (Matt. 25:41). However, there is a principle in Scripture that must be considered: Each person will spend eternity with the one they follow, whether knowingly or unknowingly. Eternity will be spent with the heavenly Father for those who have:

- Believed in Jesus and followed Him (John 3:16)
- Repented of their sins (Luke 13:3,5)
- Confessed Him openly (Rom. 10:9,10)

For those who reject Christ, eternity will be spent with the one they have followed, perhaps unknowingly, the devil.

God wants none to perish, but for all to come to repentance (2 Pet. 3:9). The choice is yours. Where will you spend eternity?

What is heaven? Who will go there?

God created heaven so that believers could spend eternity with Him, their Father. Heaven is a literal place, built by the hand of God (John 14:2; 2 Cor. 5:1; Heb. 11:10), where all who have received the salvation God has provided will eternally occupy a place of blessing and honour.

At Christ's second coming, believers will be raised with a spiritual body to meet Him and go to the place that is prepared for them:

> *For our citizenship is in heaven, from which we also eagerly wait for the Saviour, the Lord Jesus Christ, who will transform our lowly body that it may be conformed to His glorious body, according to the working by which He is able even to subdue all things to Himself.* Phil. 3:20,21

Once there, believers will be united to Jesus Christ and will partake in the marriage supper of the Lamb (Rev. 19) and the judgement seat of Christ. *"For we must all appear before the judgement seat of Christ, that each one may receive the things done in the body, according to what he has done, whether good or bad"* (2 Cor. 5:10).

Scripture declares that the church will reign with Christ and share His authority in His worldwide kingdom (1 Cor. 6:2; Rev. 1:6; 3:21; 20:4,6; 22:5). This will be an eternal testimony to God's wisdom, mercy and grace.

By revisiting Eden, we can gain a glimpse of heaven. Eden was perfectly established before Adam was ever created and placed there. If you read the account of creation in Genesis 1 and 2, you'll see that Adam was created on the sixth day of creation. Remember, God rested on the seventh day, so man came on the scene near the end of God's activity.

When God placed Adam in the garden, He told the man to tend or keep it, not establish it. God provided everything Adam could ever want or need, including one like him, Eve. God was present and visited with Adam and Eve in the garden in the cool of the evening.

Heaven is a complete, perfect place where believers will spend eternity with God. However, unlike Eden, those present are there either because of decisions they made during life on earth or because they were too young to make a decision. Every tear will be wiped away there, no serpent will be there to tempt, and no sin or despair will separate people from God.

Life in heaven will be unlike anything experienced here. Paul wrote: *"Now we see things imperfectly as in a poor mirror, but then we will see everything with perfect clarity. All that I know now is partial and incomplete, but then I will know everything completely, just as God knows me now"* (1 Cor. 13:12 NLT).

Choose today where to spend eternity. Jesus said that to enter heaven, we must do the will of the Father (Matt. 7:21). Nevertheless, *"If we confess our sins, He is faithful and just to forgive us our sins and to cleanse us from all unrighteousness"* (1 John 1:9).

What is the difference between the kingdom of God and the kingdom of heaven?

Jesus told His disciples—all believers—to seek first the kingdom of God and His righteousness (Matt. 6:33). Jesus also told a man named Nicodemus that unless he was born again, he couldn't see the kingdom of God (John 3:3). These references, and others like them, demonstrate that the kingdom of God in this present age is a spiritual, heavenly kingdom, not an earthly one.

Many followers of Jesus during His ministry on earth were confused by this concept of the kingdom. They wanted an earthly kingdom that would overthrow Roman rule, but Jesus ushered in a heavenly kingdom that was present in His followers only.

The teachings of Jesus regarding the kingdom of heaven and the kingdom of God are recorded in three of the four Gospels—Matthew, Mark and Luke. The characteristics of the kingdom of God and the kingdom of heaven are basically the same and are taught in nine parables of Jesus:

- The soils (Matthew 13:1-23; Luke 8:4-8)
- The weeds (Matthew 13:24-30,36-43)
- The virile seed and the fertile earth (Mark 4:26-29)
- The mustard seed (Matthew 13:31,32; Mark 4:30-32)
- The leaven (Matthew 13:33)
- The hidden treasure (Matthew 13:44)
- The pearl of great value (Matthew 13:45,46)
- The net (Matthew 13:47-50)
- Treasure old and new (Matthew 13:52)

The Jews expected the promised Messiah to establish an earthly, political kingdom when He came. However, Jesus came as the Lamb of God that takes away the sin of the world, and offered salvation to all, both Jew and Gentile alike.

Jesus said, *"My kingdom is not of this world"* (John 18:36) and that the kingdom of God is within us (Luke 17:21). He taught that the kingdom of God is spiritual and we enter by being born again (John 3:2,3,5). Paul declared: *"For the kingdom of God is not meat and drink; but righteousness, and peace, and joy in the Holy Ghost"* (Rom. 14:17 KJV).

Christ will establish an earthly, political kingdom at His second coming, which will be the material realization of the promises given in the Old Testament. Those who have accepted Jesus as their personal Saviour and Lord will reign with Christ in this kingdom (Rev. 20).

Who are the 144,000 mentioned in the book of Revelation?

Revelation 7:4-8 mentions 144,000 who were *"sealed"* unto Christ and Revelation 14:1-5 mentions 144,000 who *"follow the Lamb wherever He goes."* As you will discover, these passages refer to two different groups of people.

Revelation 7:4-8 says there will be 144,000 representing the 12 tribes of Israel—12,000 from each tribe. We know they are still on the earth because Scripture goes on to describe another group, obviously comprised of millions of people:

> *After these things I looked, and behold, a great multitude which no one could number, of all nations, tribes, peoples, and tongues, standing before the throne and before the Lamb, clothed with white robes, with palm branches in their hands, and crying out with a loud voice, saying, "Salvation belongs to our God who sits on the throne, and to the Lamb!"* Rev. 7:9,10

The 144,000 descendants of the tribes of Israel will become the most effective witnesses for Jesus during the brief period just prior to the physical return of the Lord. They will come from each corner of the earth, so will be able to witness in the native languages of the people.

These faithful witnesses will preach the Gospel of Christ to a world caught in the grip of the great tribulation during which the rulers of darkness and the Antichrist will seek to deceive and destroy all humankind.

"Then I looked, and there before me was the Lamb…and with Him

144,000 who had His name and His Father's name written on their foreheads" (Rev. 14:1 NIV). These 144,000 are with the Lamb and follow Him wherever He goes. This group has believed in the One of whom John the Baptist spoke when he said, *"Behold! The Lamb of God who takes away the sin of the world!"* (John 1:29).

The Lord has redeemed these saints from "among men" and drawn them unto Himself. That they have been redeemed shows their status as followers of Jesus. Scripture says they are offered as firstfruits to God and the Lamb (Rom. 8:23; James 1:18).

The 144,000 are believers who have faithfully carried the name of Christ to their world. Let us be as valiant in our testimony and so share with them in the joy of the Lord.

What is the new covenant?

T he Jewish prophet Jeremiah wrote the following words hundreds of years before the birth of the Son of God in Bethlehem:

> *"Behold, the days are coming," says the Lord, "when I will make a new covenant with the house of Israel and with the house of Judah—not according to the covenant that I made with their fathers in the day that I took them by the hand to lead them out of the land of Egypt, My covenant which they broke, though I was a husband to them," says the Lord. "But this is the covenant that I will make with the house of Israel after those days," says the Lord: "I will put My law in their minds, and write it on their hearts; and I will be their God, and they shall be My people. No more shall every man teach his neighbour, and every man his brother, saying, 'Know the Lord,' for they all shall know Me, from the least of them to the greatest of them," says the Lord. "For I will forgive their iniquity, and their sin I will remember no more."*
> Jer. 31:31-34

This is God mediating a new covenant with His creation. A covenant is the most solemn and binding agreement into which two parties can enter. The new covenant, or New Testament, is fulfilled in Jesus Christ, the Son of God.

The writer of Hebrews 8 was inspired by the Holy Spirit to quote Jeremiah's prophecy of the new covenant. Hebrews 12:24 states that Jesus is the Mediator, the "go-between" or "intervening one," who effects agreement of the new covenant, which is founded on better promises (Heb. 7:20-28).

The writer to the Hebrews declared, *"... You have come to God...to Jesus the Mediator of a new covenant, and to the sprinkled blood that speaks a better word than the blood of Abel"* (Heb. 12:23,24 NIV). Cain murdered Abel, the second son of Adam. Abel's blood cried for vengeance, but Jesus' blood cries for salvation for all.

When Jesus came, died on the cross and then victoriously rose again, He provided for all mankind a way by which they may receive forgiveness of sin and salvation through repentance and faith in Him (John 3:16; Rom. 3:23; 6:23; Eph. 2:8,9).

During the Lord's supper, Jesus spoke of His blood of the new covenant, which is *"shed for many for the remission of sins"* (Matt. 26:28). Under the old covenant, God's people worshipped Him through obedience to the law. However, in the new covenant, Christ fulfilled the law (Matt. 5:17) and now dwells within believers by the Holy Spirit.

Jesus' sacrificial death and our receiving His promise of salvation allow entry into the kingdom of heaven. Jesus came to give us life more abundantly (John 10:10). Part of giving life is overcoming death, and we know that He overcame death because of the empty tomb. Therefore, the same life that is in Him is in every believer. All who receive Jesus as Saviour and Lord will be raised to eternal life with Him.

The Crossroads Ministry Story

It All Began In 1962...

In Pembroke, located in the Ottawa Valley of north-eastern Ontario, David Mainse was the pastor of an area church. It was there, in 1962, David and his wife Norma-Jean first broadcast the Gospel on black and white TV sets. The program was called *Crossroads.*

As the Mainse family moved to other centres to pastor, the television ministry moved with them. It grew in popularity and was aired on more and more stations.

In 1977, the ministry of Crossroads launched daily programming across Canada from God-given facilities in downtown Toronto at an address after which the telecast was named: ***100 Huntley Street.***

Crossroads' Mission Statement

"The key objective of Crossroads Christian Communications Incorporated is to add to and bring unity to the body of Christ through direct and indirect evangelism; to enhance and augment the ministry of the local church; and to build understanding, credibility and attractiveness of life in Jesus Christ.

"This will be accomplished by the creative use of television and other media, together with other activities which respond to the mission conscience and needs of the constituency. The responsibility for outreach is to the world. Outside North America, C.C.C.I. responds only to the requests from organized and established Christian leadership. The role is as a catalyst to the development of indigenous and self-supporting ministry."

Accountability

Crossroads Christian Communications Inc. is federally chartered in both Canada and the United States as a charitable, non-profit organization. As such, it is funded wholly through free-will offerings. Crossroads is audited annually by Price Waterhouse Lybrand. Financial statements are available upon written request.

Crossroads receives the annual Seal of Financial Accountability from the Canadian Council of Christian Charities.

David & Norma-Jean

Lorna

Norm

Ron & Ann

Cal

Reynold & Kathy

The Crossroads Ministry

is made possible through the generous gifts of people like you who believe in Life-Changing Television. As many as 1.5 million individuals tune in to the *100 Huntley Street* broadcast every week.

24-Hour Prayer Ministry

Prayer lines are available 24 hours a day – a lifeline for many in crisis.

Crossroads receives calls from over 30,000 needy people each month. Over 200 volunteer prayer partners donate 30,000 hours each year to minister and pray for such needs as salvation, healing, substance abuse, suicide, emotional problems and family concerns.

Crossroads also provides helpful ministry materials on many relevant subjects like anger, depression, grief, healing, reconciliation, etc.

To help new Christians become firmly established in their relationship with God, Crossroads uses in-depth Bible study courses. New Christians are also encouraged to join a local church for further spiritual growth and fellowship with other believers.

Crossroads Prayer Lines

A Crossroads prayer partner would love to pray with you for any special need you may be facing today. Simply call our prayer line nearest you:

Vancouver, BC	**604-430-1212**
Calgary, AB	**403-284-4721**
Edmonton, AB	**780-944-0742**
Regina, SK	**306-781-8970**
Winnipeg, MB	**204-949-9414**
Burlington, ON or USA	**905-335-0100**
Toronto, ON	**416-929-1500**
Montreal, QC	**514-935-8814**
Quebec City, QC	**418-864-7448**
Saint John, NB	**506-674-2400**
Halifax, NS	**902-455-2600**
St. John's, NF	**709-738-2731**

Hearing impaired TDD 905-335-6104

A Special Invitation: If you live in the Toronto/Burlington area and would like to join the ministry as a prayer partner, call the National Ministry Centre at:
905-332-6400, ext. 2383

The Geoffrey R. Conway School of Broadcasting and Communications

Twice each year, Crossroads conducts a unique, 16-week course. This fully-accredited course in Christian television production is designed especially to prepare those with a vision to start Christian programming in their own countries. Crossroads has trained over 1,350 students from 70 countries thus far.

Circle Square Ranches

Circle Square Ranches are Christian camping centres dedicated to meeting the needs of Canada's children and youth. Our western-style facilities bring the pioneering spirit of the old west into the 21st century, making each summer at Circle Square Ranch an unforgettable experience. Our nine ranches are committed to "steering our nation's youth in the right direction."

Call the ranch nearest you at:
1-800-539-9598

Crossroads' Emergency Response and Development Fund

This is a fund established out of compassion for people in areas of the world hit by disasters such as earthquakes, famine and war. Crossroads has sent millions of dollars in relief to the world's needy.

The Walk of Faith

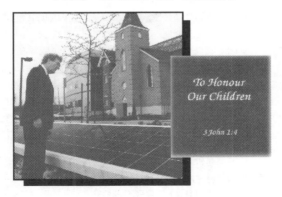

To Honour
Our Children

3 John 1:4

The Walk of Faith is a lovely walkway around the Crossroads Centre. Along the walkway are engraved granite stones which have been donated in honour or in memory of special people. Find out how you can join the Walk of Faith by calling: **1-800-265-3100**

Other Crossroads TV Outreaches Sharing The Love of Jesus...

Rise & Shine
A morning breakfast show with news and inspiration.

Nite Lite
Middle-of-the-night open-line ministry.

T.O.
Saturday morning children's programming with a positive message.

The NIRV
Teens reaching teens with music and discussion.

Visit The Crossroads Centre

Here is a "to do" list of special Crossroads activities:

- ✔ Join our live studio audience for *100 Huntley Street*
- ✔ Tour the Crossroads Centre
- ✔ Enjoy a special presentation in the Promise Theatre
- ✔ Stay for lunch at the Towne Square Café
- ✔ Browse in The Village Shoppe bookstore
- ✔ Join our annual tour to the Holy Land

For further information and reservations,
call the Visitor Care department at:
905-332-6400, ext. 1281

**1295 North Service Road, P.O. Box 5100,
Burlington, Ontario, Canada, L7R 4M2
Phone: 905-335-7100**

Visit the Crossroads internet homepage at:
www.crossroads.ca

Or send an e-mail message to: **huntley@crossroads.ca**